SUSIE KING TAYLOR

RISE. RISK. REMEMBER.
INCREDIBLE STORIES OF COURAGEOUS BLACK WOMEN

SUSIE KING TAYLOR

Nurse, Teacher & Freedom Fighter

Erica Armstrong Dunbar & Candace Buford

Aladdin

New York London Toronto Sydney New Delhi

ALADDIN

An imprint of Simon & Schuster Children's Publishing Division
1230 Avenue of the Americas, New York, New York 10020
First Aladdin paperback edition September 2023
Text copyright © 2023 by Erica Armstrong Dunbar
Cover illustration copyright © 2023 by Lisbeth Checo
Reminiscences of my life in camp with the 33d United States colored troops, late 1st S. C. volunteers
by Susie King Taylor was originally published in 1902. Credit line: Library of Congress.
Source: https://www.loc.gov/item/02030128
Also available in an Aladdin hardcover edition.
All rights reserved, including the right of reproduction in whole or in part in any form.
ALADDIN and related logo are registered trademarks of Simon & Schuster, Inc.
For information about special discounts for bulk purchases, please contact Simon & Schuster
Special Sales at 1-866-506-1949 or business@simonandschuster.com.
The Simon & Schuster Speakers Bureau can bring authors to your live event.
For more information or to book an event contact the Simon & Schuster Speakers Bureau
at 1-866-248-3049 or visit our website at www.simonspeakers.com.
Cover designed by Karin Paprocki
Interior designed by Mike Rosamilia
The text of this book was set in Perpetua.
Manufactured in the United States of America 0823 OFF
2 4 6 8 10 9 7 5 3 1
Library of Congress Control Number 2023933948
ISBN 9781665919944 (hc)
ISBN 9781665919937 (pbk)
ISBN 9781665919951 (ebook)

This book is dedicated to teachers.
Their skill and dedication
promise a better tomorrow.
—E. A. D. and C. B.

Authors' Note

Dear Reader,

Hello and welcome to what we know will be an incredible and powerful reading experience! We are honored to introduce Susie Baker King Taylor, who at the age of fourteen, risked everything to fight for freedom and to break the bonds of enslavement for millions of other Black Americans. She was a freedom seeker, a teacher, a nurse, and supporter of the Union troops during the Civil War.

Susie King Taylor tells us that she was born "under the slave law in Georgia" on August 6, 1848, and over the course of her sixty-four years, she witnessed bondage, freedom, and segregation. Unlike most people living under slavery, Susie King Taylor could trace her family tree back to her great-great-grandmother, who watched five of her sons participate in the American Revolution. The women in Taylor's family were strong and unique, and it is not surprising that she followed suit.

Taylor is best known for her service to the Union Army during the Civil War, where she taught, nursed, and supported Black soldiers. She worked alongside the First South Carolina Volunteer Infantry (later known as the 33rd United States Colored Infantry Regiment). These soldiers were among the first Black men to volunteer their lives to fight for the Union Army. Taylor accompanied these men during the war and became known as one of the first African Americans to teach at a freedmen's school in Georgia—all while she was a teenager. She nursed sick soldiers, held the hands of dying men, learned how to clean and fire weapons, and laundered the clothing of soldiers. Unlike the men who fought for the Union, she would never receive payment for her work.

We made the decision to write this book about Susie King Taylor's experiences in a first-person voice. Connecting the information given to us from her own narrative that she published in 1902, we have included additional experiences we imagine must have confronted her. In a few places, we needed to create first names to breathe life and dignity into the people who lived during this time. In some cases, we use "informed speculation"—meaning we tried to estimate what Taylor would have experienced—even though she may not have told us about her feelings in her writing. Even so, this is a history book, and wherever possible, we use Susie King Taylor's own words. We have included the primary source (her own writing) at the end of this text, and we invite you to compare and contrast our telling of Taylor's life with her own

Reminiscences of My Life in Camp. It is the only known account of the experiences of Black Civil War soldiers written by a Black woman.

Reminiscences includes terms that were acceptable when Susie King Taylor was alive but are no longer appropriate. Words such as "colored" and "negro" are terms that are now seen as offensive, and we decided to remove them from our book wherever possible. We substituted these words with terms such as "Black" and "enslaved" in order to give dignity and respect to the people who were forced into bondage against their will. We ask that readers move through this language with an ethic of care.

Susie King Taylor took risks so that she and her loved ones could experience the power and the responsibilities of freedom. We can think of no better time to introduce her story, and we hope that all who read these words will celebrate her courage.

—Erica Armstrong Dunbar &
Candace Buford

Chapter 1

MY GRANDMOTHER DOLLY WORKED AS A laundress in the city of Savannah, Georgia. I didn't tell her how much I admired her, because that's not the kind of thing you say to your grandma, but I studied her every day—watching her work hard washing clothes, cleaning boarding rooms, and trading supplies. She earned her own money, and this was no small feat for a Black woman born enslaved in 1820. Unlike most, Grandma managed to find her way off the plantation in Liberty County, Georgia, and she settled thirty-five miles away in the city. It was hard to make ends meet, but it gave her the opportunity to get paid for her work, and she managed to squirrel away a nice bit of money. Grandma had carved out a nice little half-life for herself, somewhere between slavery and freedom. I was lucky to have her.

Most mornings she rose early, hours before she roused me and my siblings from slumber. She said it was so she could work in peace without having children underfoot. But as I grew older and could no longer be classified as a child, she still let me sleep. I came to the conclusion that she wasn't just protecting her workflow but also some semblance of childhood for us, as children who weren't commanded to work. She prayed for a better life for us—one far away from the fields of Grest Farm, where we could have just a tiny bit more time to dream.

I had been living in that small Savannah home with her since I was seven years old. In 1856, Grandma convinced Mr. Grest to let me and two of my siblings live with her in the city, away from the plantation, where my thoughts had room to roam. Sometimes, when I was sure no one was looking, I thought about a world in which no man could say he owned another person. I dreamed of freedom.

That seed of freedom took root.

If Mr. Grest ever knew what I was thinking, he would have never allowed me to live with my grandmother. But he did not own my thoughts. Those were tucked safely away in my mind—which was a good thing too, because my mind was swimming with words and stories from all the books I could read now.

The old floorboards creaked underneath Grandma's weight as she shuffled across the tiny house and made her way to her washboard, which was leaning against the back door. Her gaze craned toward the room where my little sister and brother and I slept. For a moment, I was sure she could see me watching her through half-closed eyes. But she smiled contentedly at the sound of muffled snores, then turned and carefully peeled her apron off its hook.

She wrapped the drawstrings behind her back, then drew them forward again. A heavy sigh escaped her wrinkled lips, puckering the skin of her weathered cheeks—all signs of excessive exposure to Georgia's hot sun, making her look a little older than her thirty-eight years of age. Grandma was a good-sized woman, five feet seven inches tall with a rich dark complexion, similar to many of us who were born or lived near coastal Georgia. She opened the back door, and the porch groaned under her weight as she started her daily chores.

I unfolded myself from my younger sister and brother sleeping next to me on our pallet. My brother stirred, and I thought his eyes would flutter open, but he rolled over and curled into the covers.

I climbed over my siblings and walked to the fireplace, where a pot of water was simmering above the hearth. Grandma's mug rested beside the stool. Shavings of dried sassafras roots lined the bottom of it. She swore by her tea— she drank it every morning, said it warded off all sickness and infection and kept her vitality up. I was wiping down another mug so that I could have some tea too, when the back door opened again.

"Child, what are you doing up?" she tutted under her breath. But by the way her eyebrows turned up, I could tell she was relieved to see me. "Give me a hand with these, please?"

She opened her apron, revealing dozens of eggs she'd collected from the coop, then carried them to the table. I sprang up from my perch near the fireplace, the tea in my grandmother's mug sloshing droplets onto the floor as I rushed to help her.

"This is a great haul," I said as I dove my hand into the bundle. Grandma's shoulders rumbled as she chuckled—she was clearly pleased with the amount of goods she had to sell.

I set the eggs in a wicker basket, careful not to smash any. Underneath the eggs were a few bunches of carrots from the garden—vibrant in color and healthy-looking—that would fetch a good price at the market. Grandma pulled out a second basket from underneath the table and diverted some of the produce into it.

"These are for today's market," she said with a smug smile, admiring her surplus. "And I guess we'll need to gather the other things I put aside for Shakespeare—he'll be here early tomorrow morning, and I want to be ready for him." She gestured to the bundle of twine on the table, which she used to package the bacon, tobacco, flour, molasses, and sugar that she purchased and brought back to the plantation every three months. Grandma would visit with my mother and then trade with people in the neighboring places for eggs, chickens, or cash, if they had it. She would carry everything back to the Savannah market, where she had a customer who sold them for her. The profit from these, together with laundry work and care of some bachelors' rooms, made a good living for her. Since there were no railroad connections between the plantation and Savannah, and all travel was by stagecoach, she hired a wagon, and Shakespeare was the coachman.

"I wonder how long his beard will be this time," I mused as I picked up a bundle of bacon. I used to visit the stable where Shakespeare kept his horses on Barnard Street, just so I could look at his signature bushy beard that nearly reached his knees.

"You know he doesn't like people fussing over his beard." Grandma planted her hands on her hips and surveyed the table; then her eyes wandered to the porch, where her big pot of water was surely beginning to boil. "I don't know how I'll finish cleaning the bachelor's rooms and doing the washing before the end of the day. But I'mma sure try."

"I'll help you. Don't worry." I slid the mug of sassafras tea to her end of the table.

"Well . . ." She sighed, looking at the sprawl of goods on the table. She took a sip of her tea, then smacked her lips with satisfaction. "Perhaps you could lend me a hand after school? Oh! That reminds me. . . ."

She shuffled to her satchel by the door and pulled out an item wrapped in brown paper. I recognized the shape and heft of it instantly.

"A *book?*" I gasped, reaching out for it, eager to discover the secrets inside. I wanted to learn above all else. But my elated surprise quickly curdled to fear, and I dropped the book on the floor.

I was the property of Mr. Grest of Grest Farm—tied to that family for life, fated to toil on their land for their spoils. Reading was forbidden for the enslaved, and the consequences were severe. If caught, I could be fined and publicly whipped, alongside whoever taught me.

I scrunched up my eyebrows. "How did you get this?"

"Never you mind where I got it." She mumbled something about how I was *old enough to know better than to ask such questions*, then took another sip of her special brew. And she was right. At ten years old, I was old enough to know a lot of things—like the fact that an enslaved person in possession of a book was a punishable offense. But my grandmother believed the risks outweighed the benefits, so she had enrolled me and my brother in a secret school.

"You can supplement your schooling with that. Read something new for a change. I see your Bible getting more worn out by the day."

Books were expensive—so expensive that we only had three in the house. I wondered how she'd gotten this book, how much it had cost, and if anyone had seen her buy it, but even as I worried over its journey into my hands, I cracked it open and leafed through the first pages. I couldn't help it. I was drawn to the words.

"What does that say?" She tapped her finger on the top of the page.

"Charles Dickens—I guess that's the author's name. It's a book about Christmas. Do you think it's a real story?"

"I'd have to ask . . . oh, never you mind. Help me get more eggs from the coop. And there's jam that needs canning for the market. And—and this is important—don't let anyone see that book. Your mother would never forgive me if I let anything happen to you."

Her dark eyes grew distant. Our life here was a tenuous one where we had one foot in the city and another one tied to the plantation. One misstep, and we'd be back on the farm, surely working the fields.

"No one will know." I gripped my grandmother's hand and hid the book under a loose kitchen floorboard. I left the kitchen and quietly walked over to my brother's side of the bed, and I roused him from his blankets. My little sister could sleep longer, but it was time for my brother to get ready for school.

We walked down Bay Lane, our schoolbooks crinkling under our clutches. I had wrapped them in paper, as I always did before our trek to the widow Mrs. Woodhouse, a free woman who lived between Habersham and Price Streets, about half a mile from our house. No one could know we were attending school.

I could handle a secret. I was *old enough to know better*

than to run my mouth. Or at least that's what my grandmother told me.

My brother stopped and bent down to pick up a laurel leaf in his path. He twirled the stem between his fingers.

"This one's good. I'll add it to the others. I'm gonna make a crown like that Julius Caesar."

"Hush." I tugged on his sleeve, eager for him to hurry up. We were not at my grandmother's house, where we could speak more freely. We were in public, half a mile away from the relative safety of home. And there were white folks around. It was my responsibility to look after my brother and sister, especially when we were away from Grandma.

"Don't say anything about Caesar until we get into Mrs. Woodhouse's."

We had paper-wrapped books so that white folks, and especially the police, wouldn't see them. Anyone holding a book who looked like me meant trouble, or at least that's what most white folks thought. But we only wanted to learn, same as everybody else.

"But—"

"No buts." I shook my head. He was young, but that didn't matter. He knew better. I leaned against a tree near the corner of Bay Lane and Habersham Street. Tucking my book underneath my arm, I straightened his collar and patted it flat. The white shirt wasn't much to look at—sort of tattered and browning under the armpits. But at least he had a shirt, a decent pair of trousers, and shoes. Some of the kids at school came barefoot. I took pride in our clothing, threadbare as it was. "Go on inside. I'll be in shortly."

My brother nodded, then turned on his heels. He was used to this process. We entered Mrs. Woodhouse's house one at a time, so as not to raise any unnecessary suspicion. Sometimes the neighbors saw us trickling into the house, but they assumed we were learning trades. Because we were enslaved, we weren't supposed to learn how to read and count.

But we did anyway. Grandma insisted on it.

I counted to sixty under my breath, trying to blend in with the people milling about. Then I slipped through the gate and walked through the small yard.

The back door was slightly ajar. It creaked as I opened it slowly and stepped into the kitchen. I closed it behind me, leaving it the same way I found it. There was another student somewhere out there, counting to sixty just like I did before they could come inside.

I placed my book on a desk at the end of the L-shaped kitchen, which served as our school room. There were about thirty of us crammed into the small space, all chatting in hushed tones. The talking quieted as soon as Mrs. Woodhouse's daughter, Ms. Mary Jane, bustled through the hallway door. She was dressed in a faded but tasteful plaid dress. She was also a free woman like her mama, and she carried her chin high and her shoulders squared.

I would stand as proud as they did if I was free and had a

house of my own. I liked the sound of that. I wanted that kind of freedom, I thought, looking out the window. When I was finally free, I'd teach just like the Woodhouse women.

Ms. Mary Jane cleared her throat and shimmied through the tightly packed room, balancing a stack of weatherworn books in her skinny brown arms.

"All right, y'all, listen here." She leaned against the counter, smiling so wide that a dimple formed in her cheek. "We're going to be reading the Book of Exodus today. It's all right if you don't have a Bible. I have a few extras. Some of y'all might have to share."

She grabbed a copy from her stack of well-worn Bibles and wiggled it in the air. A few students raised their hands, jostling to grab one of the extra copies. Some faces in the room were new. Their wide eyes and hesitation made me wonder if this was their first time in school.

Ms. Mary Jane handed one of the new students a Bible, a girl about my age. The girl's eyes widened as she wrapped her fingers around the book, then her jaw slackened with what looked like a little wonder and a little fear. I remembered feeling the same way when I touched my first book—eager to read but so scared to be caught with a book.

"Find a partner who can help you, okay, little ma'am?" Ms. Mary Jane scooted the girl toward the rest of the beginner readers near the front corner.

"I can help, ma'am," I said from the back of the kitchen.

"I know you can." She smiled with her approval. She gestured to the front of the kitchen where the newcomers were congregating. "Help the little ones, will you? I've got this group."

"Yes, ma'am." I nodded, then slid past her as I made my way to the other side of the room.

I held my arms wide, corralling the early readers into a corner, carving out our space to learn. I liked teaching the young ones. Shoot, I liked teaching older pupils too. There was power in knowledge—that's what my grandmother always said. And I liked the idea of more people who looked like me knowing their letters. It made me feel less alone in the world, like I had a community.

Carefully I unwrapped my book. I set the paper at my feet instead of throwing it away. I'd need it to wrap my book back up at the end of school. Paper was precious because it was expensive, and I needed to make the best of this sheet for as long as possible.

Halfway through the lesson, Mrs. Woodhouse walked in. I had great respect for this woman, and the twinkle in her eye always made me smile.

"Susie," she said as she approached my pod of students. She folded her arms, that twinkle in her eyes gleaming. "I see you're teaching again."

"Yes, ma'am. I don't mind, though."

"I know you don't. But I do have a treat for you." She crouched, her knees creaking as she lowered to my eye level. "A friend of mine, Mrs. Mary Beasley, said she can teach you more than what you're learning here."

"But I like it *here*." I took a step back, fear swelling in my chest. I didn't want to leave the familiar schoolhouse that had taught me everything I knew.

"Child, don't be scared. This is a good problem to have. I've taught you everything I know, and my daughter has taught you everything she knows. Wouldn't it be nice to move up in your schooling? You'd advance your reading and needlework and such."

"Yes," I said. I didn't want to leave this homey, makeshift schoolhouse, but I did want to learn more—so much more.

"Mrs. Beasley is actually in the next room and very eager to meet you. Would you like to come introduce yourself? The little ones will be all right for now." Mrs. Woodhouse heaved herself upward from her crouch and cocked her head at her daughter. "Would you mind taking over Susie's students for a spell?"

"Um." Ms. Mary Jane blinked, looking somewhat overwhelmed. She gave a reluctant nod. "Yes, ma'am."

"Wonderful!" Mrs. Woodhouse clasped her hands together. She gave me a small wink before turning to the hall door. Over her shoulder she said, "Follow me."

When we entered the small sitting room, Mrs. Beasley was standing next to the fireplace, wearing a fine gown of navy blue with a pressed bow across the chest—the kind Mrs. Grest would special-order from the shops in the city. Her curls were fastened in a loose bun atop her head. She stepped forward, her skirt swishing against the wooden floor.

"You must be Susie. I've heard such splendid things about you." She held her hand out between us, waiting for me to shake it. I stood there, suddenly too shy to move. Mrs. Beasley was unlike any woman I'd ever met before. It was uncommon for a woman to shake hands, especially with a child. I blinked up at Mrs. Woodhouse, who nudged me forward.

"Nice to meet you, ma'am," I said under my breath. I gripped the tips of her fingers and meekly shook her hand.

"No need to be timid." Mrs. Beasley gripped my fingers a little tighter, her smile widening. "I hear your reading comprehension is impeccable, and you show promise with arithmetic."

"Yes, ma'am." I rolled the word *impeccable* around in my head, trying not to forget it. I'd write it down in my tattered notebook later. I had a collection of good words, and something told me if I stuck with Mrs. Beasley, I'd fill my notebook up in no time.

"Would you like to continue your studies with me? Perhaps learn about geography along with some more literature?" She tilted her head to the side, her eyes tightening slightly. "The choice belongs to you."

I frowned, so unsure. No one had ever given me a firm choice to make. Free will wasn't something I was used to. In this world of enslavers who held people in bondage, I was usually told what I had to do. But in this moment, I was given power, the power to choose. I couldn't let this opportunity slip away, so I stood up straighter, squaring my shoulders like Ms. Mary Jane.

"I would like that very much, thank you. And . . ." I stepped forward, feeling bolder. "I would like to read Shakespeare. I know a man named Shakespeare who has a long beard and drives a stagecoach, and he told me there are legendary stories written by a man of that same name. And I would like to know why folks call people from the North Yankees. And what is an abolitionist? And . . ."

"Hush, child." Mrs. Woodhouse squeezed my shoulder hard. Her eyes widened in horror as she met Mrs. Beasley's gaze. I got the impression that I'd said a very dangerous word. But instead of looking as concerned as Mrs. Woodhouse, Mrs. Beasley raised a curious brow. I thought I heard a small chuckle escape her lips.

"Not so timid after all. Good." Mrs. Beasley flared her nostrils as she folded her arms. She appraised me for a moment. "I'm not sure how much I can teach you. You may soon surpass my lessons."

I blinked up at her, confusion swirling in my mind. I had only just agreed to learn under Mrs. Beasley's tutelage.

What came after Mrs. Beasley?

"I'll settle it with your grandmother. You'll start next week if it suits." Mrs. Woodhouse placed her hand on my back and gently pushed me toward the kitchen door. "Now, go on and get back to your work."

When the school day was over, I grabbed the discarded paper off the floor and rewrapped my book. My younger brother did the same. Then we left the way we'd entered, slipping one by one through the back door. I waited for my brother about a block away from the house, near the old water pump. Then together we marched down the road, a bit quieter than we were on our journey there. I was deep in thought, thinking about Mrs. Beasley and her fine dress—her *impeccable* dress.

My brother gathered more laurel leaves on the way home. I even helped him this time. I only had a few more days to walk with him to school, because come next week, I was graduating to a higher learning.

Chapter 2

THE FAINT SOUNDS OF SLOSHING WATER greeted us as we approached the back of Grandma's tiny house. Grandma was elbow deep in her wooden barrel. Her sleeves were rolled up, and her white kerchief was slipping down her brow. She was leaning over the water and scrubbing a balled-up blouse against her ridged silver washboard.

She spent most of her time here on the back porch—it was the only place big enough for her laundry buckets and clotheslines. She also liked being outside, where she could keep an eye on her chickens and smell the fresh herbs that were growing in her small garden. She smiled when she saw us coming up the steps.

"Hey, babies." She straightened from her hunched position. She put her hands on her hips and pressed her thumbs into her sides, massaging her sore muscles. "I tell you, my back hurts something fierce."

"I know, Grandma." I rubbed the small of her back, trying to bring her some comfort.

"I will leave it all in God's hands." Then she leaned forward, whispering conspiratorially. "And I pray we all find freedom one day."

"Shh," I whispered, my eyes darting around the backyard to see if anyone was listening. There weren't as many white ears in this part of Savannah, but we still couldn't speak *that* freely. This was all lost on my brother, who thrust a handful of laurel leaves into her hands.

"I have enough leaves to make a crown. Look, Grandma."

"That's nice." She patted him on the head. "Y'all help me with the washing now. I'm running behind. And Bessy's gonna be here any moment for Mr. Blouis's shirts."

I inhaled sharply. Mr. Blouis was our landlord. If there was any laundry that needed to be done spick and span and on time, it was his. I grabbed an apron off the hook on the door and tied it tightly around my waist.

"These need pressing?" I asked as I slicked my hair away from my forehead and pointed to a wad of shirts on the laundering table. Grandma gave me a look—it was self-evident that these still needed to be dried before they were ironed, so I got to work, rolling my sleeves up before pinning the shirts onto the clothesline. "Mrs. Woodhouse wants a word with you when you have a chance. Says she wants to talk to you about me going to another school."

"She won't take you anymore?"

"That's not what she said." I shook my head, a sigh escaping my lips. "She just thinks I need higher education. The new teacher seems nice."

"I'll see. Long as you can still help me do the washing-up after lessons, we'll find a way to get you more schooling." She paced the small space, shoving her hands in her apron's deep pockets. Then she lowered her voice. "You listen to me— there is a power in knowledge. It's more valuable than the coins we'll get from washing these clothes. You understand?"

"Yes, ma'am."

"All right, then."

"Evening, Dolly." A voice sounded from the gate. Our heads whipped around to face the side of the yard, where the landlord's son stood. He nodded at Grandma, a small gesture of respect. It was more than most white men would do, but still less than the respect she deserved.

"Oh! Evening, Mr. James." She wiped her hands against her apron and hurried down the steps to meet him. "What can I do for you?"

"Came by to hand you this. It's a new monthly pass from Mr. Grest." He slid an envelope out of his breast pocket and handed it to her. My grandmother had carved out a half sort of freedom while living here in Savannah, but she was still at the mercy of Mr. Grest and her guardian here in the city. Both enslaved and free Black people needed passes so they could roam freely without being arrested. James placed his hat back on his head and looked over her shoulder at the laundry hanging on the line. "And while I'm here, I can also pick up the washing."

"Oh, sir. Never you mind that. Bessy will be along shortly. And I'll give it to her, don't you worry." Grandma nodded, as placating as possible.

"Oh, I don't mind waiting." He hopped up the steps and leaned against the railing, making himself quite at home. White people did things like that—they felt entitled to our space without even asking. But technically this house belonged to his father, so I guessed his intrusion was justified.

"We'll be done with it soon," I said, pressing the hot iron into his father's white shirt. His prying eyes darted to my paper-wrapped book resting on the railing's ledge. My cheeks heated, and I avoided his gaze. I swiped the book off the ledge and tucked it into my apron pocket. "It's a sewing kit," I said, looking down. "It's a gift for my mother."

The lie slipped out of me so quickly, I surprised myself. But I knew better than to run my mouth about my literacy to the landlord's son.

"It's all right, Susie." Grandma rushed up the steps, her smile tight but polite. "Tell the man how your reading is coming along."

My mouth fell open. I looked from Grandma to James and then down at the floor. I couldn't believe she'd just said that.

"So," James said, folding his arms. "How are the books I gave y'all?"

"*You* gave us the books?" I peered at him, searching for signs of jest. But he stared back at me, looking sincere and, to my annoyance, slightly amused. I lifted my chin, willing myself to look confident. I patted my apron, thumping the book in my pocket. "I haven't read the book about Christmas yet, but the Bible——I've read it twice already."

"Twice? Huh." He rubbed his chin. "Would you like another one? I got all sorts at home."

"Yes, please. Anything you can spare would be great. My reading comprehension is impeccable."

I squinted, hoping I was using my new word correctly. James's grin widened, and a laugh escaped his lips.

"Indeed." He pointed at me, still grinning.

"You're not worried about getting into trouble?" I fidgeted with my fingers in my lap. It shouldn't be a crime for me to learn to read, but it was. And on top of that, it was a crime for him to aid me in my pursuit of the written word. This was an illegal combination. If anyone found out, we'd both be punished——me most of all.

"I'm sure the authorities have bigger fish to fry." He waved his hand dismissively. Then he leaned forward, his voice quieter and more serious.

"Look, if you won't tell, I won't." He held his right hand over his heart, bowing his head solemnly.

I smiled and nodded in return.

* * *

Mrs. Beasley's parlor was narrow and long, stretching from one end of her house to the other. It was an odd sort of room, not really ideal for entertaining huge gatherings. But it was perfect for a classroom. Her writing desk sat at the end of the room with a pair of upholstered chairs facing it. It was quite the change from the packed and often chaotic L-shaped kitchen at Mrs. Woodhouse's house.

Mrs. Beasley cleared her throat, drawing my attention back to the start of the day's lesson.

"Let's try something a bit more challenging this morning," Mrs. Beasley said as she grabbed a piece of chalk off her desk. This was how she liked to teach—writing prompts on a chalkboard and having me respond on the spot. I'd been under her tutelage for almost two years now, and already we'd covered all the states and territories and the United States Constitution, and so much more. I leaned forward, curious as to what today's lesson would entail.

She held her small chalkboard on her lap as she scrawled something on it. Then she turned the board around so that it was facing me. "Can you tell me who this is?"

"That's an easy one." I slouched into my chair, my curiosity waning once I read the writing on her chalkboard. "That's James Buchanan, the president."

"That's right. And do you know his political party?"

"He is a Democrat," I said. "Isn't everyone a Democrat?" I

furrowed my brow. "I've never heard of any man calling himself anything else."

"No, Susie. Everyone is *not* a Democrat. There are Republicans too. Maybe not so much around these parts, but they do exist."

"The president is up for reelection this year, right?" I wracked my brain, remembering what I'd learned weeks ago. "The president is elected every four years, and since it's 1860, it's an election year."

"Astutely observed, Susie." Mrs. Beasley flared her nostrils, a sign that she was impressed. "But no. Normally that would be true. President Buchanan has only served one term, and traditionally, the president may run for office again if he so chooses. But he has stated that he will not run for reelection."

"Then his vice president will run?" I tilted my head and waited for confirmation. I enjoyed getting Mrs. Beasley's approval. There was something about her warm smile that lifted my spirits.

"Likely." She bobbed her head from side to side. "But there is change brewing in this country—Republican change. I hear Abraham Lincoln is doing quite well." She petered off. "You look troubled, Susie. Why is that?"

"The Republicans want to rip the country in half," I said. I'd overheard chatter all over town about the scheming tactics of Republicans.

"You can't believe everything you hear." Mrs. Beasley sighed and slouched deeper in her chair. It was odd for her to lose her composure, but something about this lesson seemed weightier and more taxing on her than the others had.

"But could it happen?" I asked in a small voice. "Could the country really be ripped in half?"

"This country is changing—bursting at the seams with all its growth, trying to forge a path to the future with the albatross of slavery around its neck. It's unsustainable." She stood from her chair and paced the length of her parlor, which doubled as her schoolroom. "The North largely wants to abandon the practice of slavery. The South wants to keep it going for as long as they can. The planting states say they're holding up the country, growing all the crops and doing all the work, and having labor of their choosing is their prerogative. But that justification doesn't hold water. It's simply not true.

"The Southern states may very well take matters into their own hands. And it's all about slavery. Don't let anybody tell you it's all about state's rights or Northern overreach or anything else like that! You hear?"

"Yes, ma'am." I nodded vigorously, surprised by her fervor.

"If Abraham Lincoln's ticket is elected, there may be trouble indeed. He's a Republican, and Lord knows how we will weather the storm of Southern Democrats. They'd rather die than give up their human property and way of life. The northern Republicans will have a fight on their hands." She brought her hand to her forehead and rubbed her temples with the tips of her fingers. "But I think what you should be asking yourself is this: Could we all really be free? Could *that* happen?"

"I hope so." I looked out the window as I envisioned such a future. "I would read a book in the park. I'd go to as much schooling as I could. And then I would open my own schoolhouse and be just like you and Mrs. Woodhouse. I'd be a teacher."

"That's flattering." She rapped her nails against my desk. "Thank you."

Then I leaned forward, eager to learn more about these Republicans preparing to take on men like Mr. Grest and the other enslavers in Savannah. I liked the sound of them.

Chapter 3

IN APRIL OF 1861, MY FRIEND KATIE O'CONNOR and I stood shoulder to shoulder, looking at Savannah's latest newspaper sprawled across her pinewood writing desk. Katie was my only white friend, and she lived the next corner over. When I'd stopped my schooling with Mrs. Beasley in 1860, James, the son of our now-deceased landlord, had agreed to give me a few lessons. Katie offered to do the same; I just had to promise never to let her father find out what she was doing. Her mother knew what was going on, but for some reason she didn't get in the way of our arrangement.

Katie stepped forward and flipped to the second page, as if further reading would temper the blow of the front-page headline, which read:

FORT SUMTER ON FIRE, THE NORTH EXASPERATED

"I can't believe they actually did it." She crossed her arms, shaking her head in disbelief. "And by the South Carolina militia, too."

"I'm as stunned as you are," I said under my breath as I scanned the page again. The South Carolina militia had attacked Fort Sumter, which was held by the federal government. The battle had lasted less than three days and ended with the militia taking control of the fort.

Southerners were angry. Within a month of Abraham Lincoln's 1860 election, Southern states had begun leaving the Union, culminating in the creation of the Confederate States of America. This attack on Fort Sumter would surely fracture the country even more than it already was.

"There were whispers of war, but I didn't expect it to actually come to pass. And so soon." Katie ran her fingers through her curls, messing up her high bun, then huffed with exasperation. "Now that the militia has stolen the fort from the Yankees, there's going to be retribution."

"What does that mean?" During my lessons with Mrs. Beasley, she'd taught me about the strength of the federal government. It seemed more formidable than the fledgling Confederacy. "Do you think South Carolina will pay for this attack?"

"The whole South will."

I ran home to share the news with Grandma. I quickly opened up the floorboard and rummaged through my small stash of books, retrieving the one with a map of the United States.

"Look here, Grandma." I pointed my finger along the map, along the coastline of South Carolina and Georgia. "There are forts all along the coast—outposts stationed in many of these sea islands. The Union Navy will come for them. It's only a matter of time. They have an impressive fleet—large gun-boats with cannons that can reach far inland."

Grandma was quiet, listening intently.

"There's one right here near Savannah," I said, tapping the page. "Fort Pulaski."

"Yes. It's less than fifteen miles from here, as the crow flies." Grandma shook her head slowly as she scanned the map. "If the Union gets that far down the coast, that means the South is in trouble."

"The North will have come to the South." I breathed softly, trying to take it all in. So many times I'd thought about the North, about how far away it was. I'd always thought freedom was over seven hundred miles away, at least. But fifteen miles away? In fifteen miles, we could run to freedom in a day or two.

The idea grew bigger in my head. It was the perfect escape plan. No one would expect a runaway to flee *south*.

"I know what you're thinking," Grandma said in a stern voice. She shook her head slowly, worry painted all over her face. "I can see it in your eyes."

"Last time I checked, my thoughts still belonged to me." I pursed my lips and turned away from her. My cheeks heated. I instantly regretted my words. I knew better than to mouth off to my grandmother.

"You better gather yourself right now," she said in a low, yet deadly serious tone. "Being a runaway is dangerous, and you are talking about things you know nothing of." She drew in a long breath and released it in a sigh. Then she paced the small space between the fireplace and the table. "And being a woman during wartime is very dangerous. Susie, listen to me. This is a dangerous time."

In that moment, I caught something in my grandmother's eyes that I didn't often see. War had come sooner than she expected, and she was scared. I was too.

Her chest deflated, and she sank into one of our creaky wooden chairs.

"I wonder if your uncle Sam will enlist." She said it in little more than a whisper, almost as if she was talking to herself. "If the Union allows us to fight, I know he will be the first to sign up."

The mention of my uncle made me pause. I thought about him, my mother and father, and my siblings back on Grest Farm. Grandma was right. Uncle Sam was a bold man, and if given the chance to fight for freedom, he would.

"Susie, the firing on Fort Sumter means *war*. That means that the reality we're used to is about to shift. You have to be extra careful."

"I'll be fine. Just as I've always been." I nodded confidently, trying to put Grandma's mind at ease. But inside, I was anything but confident. War was coming to Savannah, and by my grandmother's estimation, it would come soon.

Chapter 4

THE CANDLE FLICKERED, SENDING SHADOWS dancing across the kitchen table as my pen scrawled cursive on the page. I'd studied a copy of a pass written by Mr. Grest and taught myself how to draft convincing passes for my family and friends. The old pass I used as my template read as follows:

> SAVANNAH, GA., March 1st, 1860.
> Pass the bearer from 9 to 10:30 P.M.
> VALENTINE GREST.

Grandmother leaned so close over my shoulder that her breath brushed against my earlobe. A soft knock on the door made her breath hitch. She whipped her head around to my brother and sister and brought a finger to her lips.

"Quickly," she whispered out of the corner of her mouth.

I stashed the paper and inkwell in the stockpot on the kitchen table and put the lid on it. We couldn't be too careful. I could be hung for forging a white man's signature on a fake pass.

"Shh," she said softly as she tiptoed to the door. She cracked it open, just enough to see out with one eye. Then her shoulders relaxed, and she opened the door wider. "Come on, y'all. Quick about it. Did anyone see you?"

"No, ma'am. For if they did, I surely wouldn't be here. Not without a pass, even though it's before nine o'clock." Our neighbor, Moses, crossed the threshold, quickly shutting the door behind him. "You got the passes?"

"She's almost finished with them." Grandma looked at me over her shoulder. "Isn't that right, Susie?"

"Yes, ma'am. Won't be long now," I said, taking the paper back. I looped my *S* with a flourish, the same way Mrs. Beasley did when she wrote. It was the kind of touch that would lend these passes credibility. And they needed to be credible.

My pen faltered as I thought of my former teacher's soft smile and confident manner of speaking.

The clock tower in the town square struck eight o'clock, which meant there was only one more hour until curfew. Black people couldn't be out after dark without written permission in their pocket. When the town bell rang at nine o'clock, any Black person on the street was arrested and put in the guardhouse until the morning. Owners or guardians could then pay fines to release them. But there would be hell to pay.

I put my pen down, waving my hand over the ink to make it dry faster.

"What's it say?" Grandma asked.

"That's Mr. Grest's name." I pointed to "Valentine" on the page. "The passes are only good until ten or ten thirty p.m. for tonight. Better make it by ten, just to be safe."

"What about that month pass?" Moses asked from across the room.

"What you need a month pass for?" Grandma raised an expectant eyebrow at him.

"I don't know. It'd be nice to have just in case." He shrugged. "They say the Yankees are heading this way. They've been saying that for weeks. But this time it's true."

There was much talk about the Yankees in our circle. Every time Grandma had a visitor, it was all they could talk about. The Yanks were from the North, where things were different—at least that's what people said. And different sounded good to me. I wanted to live in a world where I didn't have to clutch a pass in my hand to walk the streets, where I didn't have to hide my books behind brown paper bags and pretend I couldn't read. I wanted all of that and more, but I was still very anxious to meet them.

"A woman at the store told me not to go near the Yankees because they would harness us to carts and make us pull the carts around in place of horses."

"That's nonsense!" Grandma flung her arms in the air,

shaking her head vigorously. "The white people don't want slaves to go over to the Yankees, and they told you these things to frighten you. Don't you see those signs pasted about the streets? A friend read them to me. One says 'I am a rattle-snake; if you touch me, I will strike!' Another reads, 'I am a wildcat! Beware.' These are warnings to the North, so don't mind what white people say."

Grandma's words matched what I had heard from my parents. They said the Yankees were going to set all the slaves free.

"Oh, how we pray for freedom!" Grandma huffed under her breath, kicking her foot up in a bit of a victory dance. She hummed a familiar church hymn under her breath. "Yes, we shall be free. Yes, we shall be free. . . ."

"Yes, we shall be free," Moses sang, his deep tenor harmonizing with my grandmother's alto. "When the Lord shall appear—"

"All right now. Quiet down. Save it for the church meeting." Grandma grabbed her shawl and slung it over her shoulders. She grabbed the door handle and looked at me before she opened the door. "You gonna be okay for a couple hours, baby?"

"We'll be fine here." I smiled reassuringly at her.

"Get some sleep. I'll be back before you know it."

"Okay, Grandma," I said as I waved goodbye.

She wrapped her tasseled shawl tightly around her shoulders and, giving me one last nod, shut the door behind her.

My bed stared back at me from the corner. Beside it,

my sister was already asleep with her corn-husk doll gripped tightly to her chest. My brother's eyelids drooped—he wasn't long from sleep. But I was wide awake.

I sank into the rocking chair near the fireplace and rocked back and forth, back and forth. These nights, when Grandma was out at her church meetings until curfew, I was always restless. That was my handwriting in my grandmother's pocket. And that was the only thing keeping her safe. It was a lot of pressure to put on my shoulders. A fresh surge of adrenaline raced through me, and I shot up from my perch. I crossed the room in two long strides until I came to the window. I peeked through the frayed curtains. The streets were quiet. Nothing was amiss.

Maybe I was anxious over nothing.

I settled back into the chair, my heart rate a little slower now. I picked up one of the last books James had gifted me and focused on its text. A yawn escaped my lips as I tried to relax. I kept waiting, like I always did when Grandma attended those church meetings of hers. Ten o'clock came and went. By the time eleven came, I knew something was wrong. The permission slips I'd written were only good until ten thirty p.m. So now Grandma was out after dark and unprotected.

I paced in the small kitchen room, biting my fingernails. My brother stirred from his cot on the far side of the room.

"What's happened?" He rubbed his eyes with the back of his hand.

"Everything is all right," I said as I shook my head, smiling tightly. "Go back to bed."

I slumped into the rocking chair near the stove with one of James's books on my lap. I was tired and struggled to keep my eyes open, even though I was worried. I could feel my eyes beginning to shut and tried to fight it.

The front door finally swung open, ripping me out of my slumber.

"Thank goodness." I clutched my chest, steadying my breathing. "I was worried."

"You were right to worry." My grandmother brought her fist to her mouth. She looked like she was about to cry. "The police came to the church meeting and took us all in."

"Was it the passes?"

"No. We were singing 'We Shall Be Free' when they came for us. They said we were planning freedom and singing 'the Lord' in place of 'Yankees.'"

"This is bad. What if Mr. Grest finds out?"

"Oh, he gonna find out surely. I sent for my guardian to come get me as soon as he could, so that I wouldn't have to spend the night in the guardhouse. Mr. Grest will know by morning." Grandma choked on a sob, then held her arms out for me to join her in a hug. "Oh, my babies! I'm so sorry."

"No," I cried into my grandmother's sleeve. "I don't want to go back to the plantation."

"I know. I know."

We held tight to each other, praying that we could remain together.

Chapter 5

SHAKESPEARE, THE COACHMAN, SHOWED up in front of Grandma's house in early April of 1862, about a week after her arrest. Given the church meeting incident and the growing tide of war, the Grest family recalled me and my siblings back to the farm. The driver hoisted my little sister onto the back of the wagon and helped my brother up too. He held his hand out to assist me, but I shook my head.

"It's okay, Shakespeare. I can pull my own weight." I slung my bag into the wagon, then heaved myself upward. I took a seat and dangled my feet off the edge of the wagon, sighing as I looked at my grandmother's house one last time.

I wasn't sure I'd ever see this place again.

"Grandma!" I yelled from the wagon as it pulled away. Her eyes tightened; I could see the love and pain swirling in her eyes. I tried to put on a brave face, holding back the tears that were welling up inside me. I didn't want the last thing she saw to be me crying.

On the outskirts of town, the floodgates opened and I cried hot, angry tears. James Blouis once told me that this war would change life as we knew it, and it would turn everything upside down. He was right. I was heading back to the farm—the last place I wanted to be. I gripped the edge of the wagon, legs bouncing with the rhythm of the bumpy road.

I felt my freedom slipping away the farther we moved away from Savannah.

April skies were a crisp blue, with just a few clouds scattered about. In the afternoon, the blue horizon darkened to gray—a stark shift in color, like a stormy squall was fast approaching. A thunderous roar that crackled through the air would always follow.

"What was that?" my sister asked, her eyebrows upturned.

"Didn't sound like thunder, that's for sure." Shakespeare looked over his shoulder, one eye on the road and one eye on us kids.

"It's not thunder," I said, listening to another roar. Those weren't rainclouds. That was smoke on the horizon, in the direction of the coast. "The Union Army must be bombing in the distance."

What a roar and din the guns made. They jarred the earth for miles. Mrs. Beasley had told me that if the Union soldiers were this far south, the Confederate Army would be in trouble.

Good.

I willed it to be true. Because when the Union Army came anywhere near Savannah, I'd be ready to run.

The road from Savannah to the farm was thirty-five miles, nearly a full day's journey. When we crossed the bridge to the island known as the Isle of Wight in Liberty County and pulled down the lane from the main road, I caught my first glimpse of the big house of Grest Farm. After being in Savannah for nearly half my life, surrounded by big, stately buildings and grand townhomes, the big house didn't look so big anymore.

Mama was waiting for us outside the cookhouse, her arms open wide to welcome us.

"Goodness! How you've grown." She tugged on the braided pigtails framing my face. "You're looking like a young woman."

"Grandma said that since I'll be fourteen soon, I'm *really* old enough to know better." I laughed.

"Did she now? That sounds like her." Mama linked her arm in mine and tugged me in the direction of the cookhouse, where she worked as a waitress and cook for the family. "And you'll live just as long as your great-great-gran. You remember how old she was?"

"Yes. She was as old as time itself." I'd heard the stories about my family many times. My great-great-grandmother was one hundred twenty years old when she died. She had seven children, and five of her boys were in the Revolutionary

War. She was from Virginia and was part Native American. She got so old, she had to be held in the sun to help her gain energy, just like a plant does when it lifts its petals to the light.

"Oh!" A shrill cry sounded from the porch, startling me. Mrs. Grest slapped both sides of her face, then ran to meet us on the gravel path. "My little Susie! Is that you, child?"

She gripped my shoulders, shuddering my stance, then she turned me around slowly so that she could have a look at me. White people always felt entitled to our space and bodies. I bit my tongue, trying not to groan.

"You grow half an inch every time I see you. Certainly can't fit at the foot of my bed anymore. Hagar Ann, how many years has it been since we let Susie go to Savannah?"

"It's been seven years, I believe," I said. My eyes locked with Mrs. Grest's for a moment too long, so I quickly looked to the ground. Ms. Mary Jane and Mrs. Beasley may have taught me to raise my chin around free folks, but it was dangerous to show such confidence in front of white people. "Apologies, ma'am."

"I asked your mama. You speak when you're spoken to, girl." Mrs. Grest's smile faltered.

"Oh, she's worn out from the journey." Mama laughed nervously. She slapped my back hard, letting me know she meant business. "She gets to talking out of turn when she's tired."

"Well, let's not let your impertinence spoil the home-coming." Mrs. Grest smiled tightly, then turned back, looking over her shoulder before stepping back into the house. "Carry on. Get changed and settled. And then we'll figure out where to put you."

As soon as she was out of sight, Mama whirled around, wearing her sternest expression.

"Have you lost your mind, talking to the missus like that?" She grabbed my arm and hurried me toward the privacy of the cookhouse.

"But Mama, I didn't mean to look her in the eyes. And it was only for a second."

"You are not in the city anymore. You're back on the plantation." Mama gripped my arm tighter, her wide eyes pleading with me to understand the severity of the situation. "She is the missus. You make her mad, and soon they'll have plans for you in the fields or worse."

I rubbed my neck. It was already aching from the mere thought of tilling the fields, and I didn't even want to contemplate what "worse" could mean. I had seen girls my age disappear from their families. In the blink of an eye, a person's life could change if an enslaver decided to sell them. I breathed deeply, reminding myself how to act on the farm.

We walked to the back kitchen, and I sat on a stool in front of the stove, watching tonight's soup simmer. My Aunt Temperance bustled in. She gave me a short nod in greeting, then cut straight to the chase.

"You've just come from Savannah, so are you going to tell us why the ground is rumbling? It's them—the Yankees, right?"

"That's them, all right." I sat up straighter, hope coursing through my veins. "They're firing on Fort Pulaski."

"Oooh!" She threw her head back and cackled just as her husband, Uncle Samuel, walked in.

"I hope they're giving them hell," he said, swiping a supper roll off the counter. He ripped off a piece and popped it in his mouth.

"They will. The fort is going to fall within days. We should be ready."

Everyone snapped their heads toward me. Their eyes grew wider in the firelight.

"Ready for *what*?" Mama asked, cocking her head to the side. "What are you suggesting?"

"That we get ready to run." Uncle Samuel stood up and walked to the other side of the kitchen counter, putting as much distance between himself and Mama as he could, because the way her nostrils were flaring, she did not look too happy with his suggestion. He held his hands up. "I've been saying it for months. We gotta take our freedom, first chance we get."

"Back in Savannah, folks said that if the Navy had made it to Pulaski, the Confederacy was in trouble. And Mama, they're here. Right now, as we speak." I winced, preemptively bracing myself for my mother's firm hand. When I opened my eyes again, she was still leaning over the counter, her lips tucked between her teeth. She was deep in thought, considering. I took a tentative step forward. "I heard the cannons roaring on the ride out here. Uncle Sam is right. It's the perfect time to run to the Union."

Uncle stepped forward, his broad shoulders squared with determination as he rounded the corner to Mama. He placed his hand atop hers, which she accepted with a reluctant sigh.

"Hagar Ann, just listen. *Listen* to me, please." His voice quivered, so he cleared his throat before continuing. "I want a better life for my family, same as you did when you sent three of your children to your mama in Savannah. I'm gonna run, and I hope you'll join us."

"I think we should head to the coast. There will be Union boats all up and down the coastline." I stroked my chin, squinting as I tried to conjure up the image of the map I had seen in my lessons. My fingers grazed the table where Mama had prepared dinner rolls; it was still coated in flour. Carefully I traced the rough outline of the coast, putting a dot where the coast was and a dot where the farm was.

"How far you reckon?" Uncle Sam asked, leaning over my shoulder to get a closer look.

"Let me think." I chewed on the inside of my cheek as I calculated the distance in my head. I met my uncle's eyes, hoping my answer wouldn't dash his hopes. "It's about twenty-five miles away."

"Would you look at that?" Aunt Tempie cupped her hand over her mouth. "The girl knows her numbers and letters and can even draw the coast. I gotta say, I'm encouraged."

"Really?" My voice hitched up a few octaves. Aunt Tempie's endorsement was a boon to both Uncle Sam and my spirits. It wouldn't be easy to get to the coast, but it was a heck of a lot closer than trekking hundreds of miles north. It was possible, and Aunt Tempie was *encouraged*. But Mama . . . by the way she was pursing her lips, she was not swayed.

"*Twenty-five miles*? My child has really lost her mind." Mama planted both her arms on the kitchen counter, looking equal parts exasperated and furious. "First she mouths off to Mrs. Grest within the first two minutes of speaking with her. And now she thinks running to the coast is gonna save her."

"Yes, but Susie is right, the Union is out there." Aunt Tempie pointed to the crude map written in flour. "And you know my husband—if he says he'll get us there, he will get us there in one piece."

"Or die trying." Uncle Sam clenched his jaw, his face growing grim. It was clear he'd been dreaming about freedom as much as I had. There was a determination in his eyes. He would not be denied this opportunity to run.

"No!" My mother threw up her hands. She shook her head slowly, then faster and faster. "No, no, no. I won't hear another word about this."

"Mama, we could be free in a day or two if we run fast enough."

"Keep your voice down. You get caught running toward the Union, you'll end up whipped or worse." She scrunched up her face, looking betrayed. "I just got you back here!"

"Hagar Ann, how many times we whisper about running to the North?" Aunt Tempie reached across the kitchen island, grazing Mama's fingers. "We just have to get close and slip behind the Union lines."

"I'm telling you, that's where freedom is," I said. "The Union Army will protect us. We just need to get there." I took another step forward, sensing my mother's softening stance on the matter. "And I can write us passes."

"You can?" She blinked in bewilderment, looking at me like she barely knew me at all.

"Do you have any paper?"

"Ain't no need for passes." Uncle Sam shuffled forward, joining our small huddle around the counter. "No white man will let us go anywhere near the Yankees, even if we show them passes. As soon as we hear the Union has taken Fort Pulaski, we gotta run."

Chapter 6

A FEW DAYS LATER, WHEN THE FIREFIGHT AT Pulaski reached a crescendo, I slipped into Mama's cabin, where she was in bed sleeping with my brother and sister. I crouched near her and placed a firm hand on her shoulder.

"Mama." I jiggled her upper arm. "Mama, wake up."

"I'm not asleep," she murmured sleepily. She rolled over to face me. "Can't you *feel* that?"

"I know." I sat there in silence for a while, feeling the earth vibrate beneath my knees. Then I squeezed her arm. "That's why we gotta run tonight. Right now."

"So you've made up your mind, have you?" Her sad eyes searched mine, probably looking for any wavering in resolve. When she didn't find any, she propped herself up on her elbows. "Get your things. Only things you can carry."

"Right." I scrambled to my feet and walked the short distance to my corner of the room, where my sack was. I shoved everything that belonged to me in the bag. I looked over my shoulder and asked, "Who's coming with us?"

"You'll go with your uncle as soon as he gives the signal."

"Wait." I paused my packing. There was something about her wording that made it sound like it was just me running. "You're not coming?"

"We can't all go, Susie. I have your brothers and sisters here, and with me and your father that makes eight of us. With Uncle Sam's family, that's fifteen people. Too obvious, too dangerous. I'll come along after you. But your uncle's right. It's not safe for you here. You gotta go now. You got a beautiful heart and mind, and I want you to protect them as much as you can, understand?"

I gripped her hands and stared into her wild, worried eyes. Almost like I was trying to drink all of her in and take her with me. I had just gotten back into her arms a week ago. Now, on the brink of leaving, I wasn't sure when I'd see her again.

I wasn't sure *if* I'd ever see her again.

"Bye, Mama." I tugged her into a hug and squeezed her tightly. My breath hitched against her shoulder as I breathed in her scent one last time. "I love you. Always."

And then, with a glance at my brother and sister, I wrenched myself free from her grasp. My chest heaved in silent mourning as I stepped into the night.

* * *

Outside the cabin, I gripped a handful of my skirts and walked as fast as I could without breaking into a jog. My satchel bobbed against my hips as I walked to my uncle's cabin.

I rapped on the door, then looked over my shoulder to see if anyone was following me. When I didn't hear a response, I knocked again.

"Uncle Sam?" I whispered in a hiss. "Uncle?"

A faint whistle caught my attention. I snapped my head in the direction of the hedgerow. The whistle sounded again, followed by a rustling of leaves. A hand popped out and motioned for me to come over.

I moved quickly.

"Did anyone see you?" Uncle Sam asked, the whites of his eyes bulging in the darkness.

"No, I don't think so." I shook my head, pretty confident in my answer.

"Where your mama at?"

"She's——" My breath hiccuped like I was about to cry. I swallowed hard, washing away the tears, then shook my head. "They aren't coming. But I'm here."

"We stick to the plan." Aunt Tempie rubbed my back in slow circles. "We'll run toward the ocean and won't stop until we reach freedom."

"Follow the smell of the sea." I grabbed the strap of my satchel, securing it tightly around my body. "That's where the Yankees will be."

I remembered what I'd learned about the Yankees. They had boats and ships, lots of them. And that's where we'd find them—on the water.

The bushes behind the cookhouse rustled.

My five cousins were there, stone still and quiet, waiting for my uncle's command.

Uncle Sam looked over my shoulder back at my family's cabin, where my mama was likely still weeping. I hoped I would turn around and see my mama, but I knew I wouldn't. When he signaled, we ran.

Our frantic strides chomped at the brush. We ran like our lives depended on it, because they did. If we got caught, Mr. Grest would know we were a family of upstarts. We'd be punished for running to the Yankees and likely be sold off somewhere deeper South, where our loved ones would never see us again.

But with freedom so close, we had to try.

I ran through the shadows, gasping for air as I pushed myself harder. With every step we took, we were getting closer to freedom, closer to the help of the Yankees. They would welcome us with open arms, would clothe and comfort us.

They had to, right? They were the good ones.

"I can't go any further." One of my cousins hunched over, gripping her knees with trembling hands. "I'm so tired."

"I know, but you gotta keep going." I tugged at her sleeve, but she ripped it out of my grasp.

"They know we're gone for sure." She shook her head, her breathing quickening. "They'll send the overseer after us. Or worse. They'll get the dogs on us."

"Then we just gotta run as fast as we can. There's no turning back now."

Chapter 7

BY FIRST LIGHT, THE TREE LINE EBBED, OPENing up to the coastline. Our feet left tracks in the sandy soil, which wouldn't do us any favors if a tracker was hot on our heels. But we were past the point of worrying—we were close to the Union. We could taste freedom. The smell of gunpowder was in the air. Every now and then, we'd cross paths with another escapee—all with the same idea we had.

Tiny islands dotted the horizon. It wasn't until we reached the shoreline that we realized our next challenge: How would we make it across the water to one of those islands? As quickly as concern appeared on my uncle's face, we spotted a man in a boat, an elderly Black gentleman who appeared to be simply waiting—for what, we didn't know. Perhaps he'd stationed himself there to help people like us make it to Union lines, or maybe it was coincidence that we'd found ourselves face-to-face with the kind-looking man? Or maybe Grandma had prayed this man into being? No matter the reason, he offered us a slow, subtle wave, inviting us onto his vessel, a blessing that none of us would ever forget.

He said nothing to us during our short journey together, and when we disembarked, he simply nodded and pointed toward a group of men huddled closely together on the beach. They carried large rifles with them and had these guns fixed toward the trees.

"Over there." I tugged on my uncle's shirt. "White folks."

"What kind of white folks?" He squinted his eyes, trying to make out the figures on the beach. "Yankees?"

"What color are their uniforms?" Aunt Tempie asked. "If they're blue, then those are the Yankees."

I squinted at the group on the beach. "They're blue." Their uniforms were unmistakably a dark blue. "Oh my goodness—we made it!"

"Come on." Uncle Sam darted in the direction of the soldiers with a lightness of foot I hadn't seen him use.

The surge of adrenaline spiked my veins, giving me a second wave of energy. It was just enough to pick up my weary feet in a sprint to the finish line.

A patrol of Union soldiers whipped around from their campfire. They looked into our frenzied eyes, pursing their lips. They didn't hold up their guns. It was like they were expecting us.

"Commander!" one of the Union soldiers yelled over his shoulder. "Looks like we have more contraband."

"Contraband?" Uncle Sam asked as he caught his breath.

"It means that you're someone else's property. But the Union doesn't recognize that. So you're kind of in limbo." He said it so cold and clinical, like it was self-evident that I was questionable property and not a human being. "And by the way, you're on St. Catherines Island now—if you didn't know."

I began to get nervous. This was not the reception I'd thought we'd receive from Union soldiers. In my mind, I'd built them up to be our guiding light who lifted us to freedom, our guardian angels. Instead, this man looked and acted like most of the white men I knew. His fellow soldier unscrewed his canteen and held it out to me.

"Would you like some water?"

"We don't have time for that." The cold soldier grabbed his sleeve, narrowing his eyes as he looked from me to the canteen. "We've been charged with reconnaissance of this island before heading back."

"It won't take but a moment." The officer pressed the water jug into my palm. "Drink up."

I tipped the canister back, and the water poured out, sloshing over the rim and onto my cheeks. But I didn't mind—I was so thirsty after running almost nonstop for close to twenty-five miles. It was a struggle to pull the water from my mouth, but I managed to pry my lips from it. I held it out to the soldier. He shifted his stance, hesitating.

"Keep it." He waved his hand dismissively. "I'll find another at camp."

I drew the canteen back, suddenly aware that he wouldn't drink after me. After a Black person touched his water, it was no longer good enough to drink. The soldier who had given it to us smiled stiffly, as if he was trying to mask the offense he'd just made.

"Did you see any Confederate soldiers on your way over here?"

"No, sir. Or we would have been captured for sure." I took a long sip of water and then another. "There's nothing in those woods but more of us, I reckon. We heard the cannons in the distance and ran for the coast."

"Happens every time. As soon as we seize a fort or advance, swarms of you people flee to us. I don't know what you think we can do."

"Take us with you." Uncle Sam brought his hands together in silent prayer. "Please?"

"Do we have room on the gunboat?" he asked his colleagues. A few of them nodded. Reluctantly, he sighed and nodded curtly. "Fine. But keep your heads down or you won't even make it to the ship. The rebs would like nothing better than to take your heads off."

The gunboat was dark, sleek, and squatty. Whoever designed this boat had done it with the intention of blending it in with the water. On the side of the boat were four square openings with cannon noses pointing out of them. And two white smoke-stacks rose from the center, huffing smoke out of the top like a chimney.

I had never seen anything like it.

The Union Army had an impressive naval fleet.

The soldiers steered our long boat alongside the naval vessel. Which was no small feat—the boat was crammed full with people, including my uncle and his family of seven and me. But we didn't complain. It was better than the alternative—being left behind on that island.

I had never been on the open water before. I'd only splashed around in the Savannah River near my grandmother's home. I didn't know how to swim, and neither did the rest of my family. I made a mental note to myself to learn how to swim. I wanted to learn how to do everything I could.

"More contraband?" an officer on deck drawled disinter-estedly. He grumbled under his breath. "We're bursting at the seams as it is."

"I'm sorry, sir." The soldier who had lent me his canteen frowned apologetically. "Would you like me to leave them behind?"

"Nonsense." A tall man in a long navy peacoat with two rows of shiny gold buttons stepped forward. His sleeves had gold stripes too, unlike the officers who had rescued us from the beach. He extended his arm and helped my aunt out of the boat. "You are most welcome with us until we get to St. Simons."

I'd heard of that island. I remembered the map that Mrs.

Beasley showed me. When she was pointing out the Union forts, she named some of the islands along the way. And St. Simons was one of the larger islands south of Savannah.

"We're moving south," I said to the man with gold stripes as he helped me onto the deck. "Is it safe?"

"This girl knows her geography." He raised his eyebrows, clearly surprised. "We captured St. Simons just one month ago, as soon as the Confederates deserted her."

"Congratulations, sir." I nodded timidly, my eyes downcast. The last time I'd looked a white person in the eyes, I'd gotten into trouble. Mrs. Grest had been shocked at my impertinence. This was an important man, and I didn't want to run afoul of him.

But this man in the navy blue coat, on the biggest boat I'd ever seen, was also shooting cannons at the rebels. I hoped he was different.

"I'm the commander of this vessel, Captain Whitmore. And what may I call you?"

"Susan Ann Baker, sir." I peeked at him through my eyelashes and then returned my gaze to the deck. "But folks call me Susie."

"Well, Susie." He nodded to my family disembarking from the long boat, then he looked out to the coastline, not far from where the patrol picked us up. "Where are you from?"

"I'm from Savannah. And that is my uncle and his family, from Grest Farm. It's not far from Savannah. Maybe thirty miles as the crow flies."

"You seem to know your way around these parts." He chuckled. "Almost like you've learned basic geography."

"Yes, of course. I know how to read a map. I can read and write too."

"Really?" His eyebrows shot up in disbelief. "Some of my men can't even read and write."

"I'm sorry to hear that," I said in a low voice. I thought briefly about offering to teach the captain's men—I'd already helped many folks learn their letters. But that would have been impertinent—no white man would want to be in an inferior situation, forced to learn from a Black girl. And I wasn't sure I even wanted to be alone with white men. That was a situation I didn't trust either.

"I have to see this literacy myself." Captain Whitmore shook his head in disbelief, then looked over his shoulder. He strode toward the desk on the deck and swiped a dip pen off the surface. With a flick of his fingers, he beckoned me to join him. The boat swayed, and my knees buckled as I made my way to his side. He dipped the pen in an inkwell, then shoved it into my unsuspecting fingers. Tapping the hard cover of the book, he said, "Write your name and where you're from on the first page."

"Okay . . ." I frowned as I cracked the book open. He obviously had his doubts, which I supposed was understand-able. I'd show Captain Whitmore that I was telling the truth. I scrawled my name in the corner of the first page, writing my cursive S with the fancy flourish Mrs. Woodhouse had taught me during our lessons. Then I placed the book into his waiting hands.

"Well, I stand corrected." His eyebrows crinkled. He looked over the rim of the book and met my gaze. "Can you sew?"

"Yes, sir. I am competent with needlework. My grand-mother taught me." I felt a pang in my chest as I thought of my grandmother. My eyes scanned the horizon to the north. Somewhere over there, the outskirts of Savannah had been bombarded. Was she all right in her tiny house in the city? My chest started to tighten as I fought back tears.

"I have some napkins and shirts that need hemming. I could certainly use your help." He raised an eyebrow at me. "I must say, Susie Ann Baker. I am rather surprised by your accomplishments. I did not know there were any Black people in the South able to read or write. You seem to be so different from the others who came from the same place you did."

"No, sir!" I replied. "The only difference is, they were reared in the country and I in the city. There was much more opportunity to learn. Is there a school on the island? I would love to help."

"A school? I don't know if—hold on." The captain drew his lips into a tight line, his eyes narrowing at a boat in the dis-tance. He snapped his head at a nearby officer. "Get everyone belowdecks. Now!"

"Captain, they appear to be hoisting a white flag."

"I've seen that before. It can't be trusted. It might be a ruse." He looked through his spyglass, his lips curling. "Please take everyone below deck. And tell the crew to be on high alert. I have a feeling this isn't a friend approaching."

Chapter 8

WE MADE OUR WAY TO THE BACK OF THE boat, where a staircase led us to the belly of the ship. Captain Whitmore said he was hiding us for our own safety. In this war between former countrymen, chance encounters were always dangerous—no one could be trusted. I appreciated his concern for our well-being.

Still, I did not enjoy the dark confines of the ship.

I'd heard stories about how our ancestors arrived in this country. They were packed tightly in the interiors of ships, forced to endure pestilence and sadness and shadows for months on end, transported as cargo, as property. As I swayed back and forth, rubbing shoulders with my family members, I wondered if we were safe at all.

"Excuse me." I slid past my uncle.

"You okay, Susie?"

"Yes, I'm fine." I stood near a small circular porthole, trying to see what was happening and why we needed to hide.

The small raft approached my side of the ship. As it drew nearer, I could make out one white man about the same age as Captain Whitmore. The man had graying in the beard but didn't look too old. I leaned closer to the window so that I could hear what was going on.

"What is your business, sir?" one of the soldiers inquired.

"My name is Mr. Edward Donegall. I'm looking for my two servants," the man yelled up to the soldiers on deck. His eyebrows arched inward as he continued to plead. "Their names are Nick and Judith. Perhaps you've come across them?"

"I'm sorry, sir. I know nothing about them." It was the captain's voice that boomed over the water. I recognized its timbre.

"You must return them to me." The man on the small boat crossed his arms. "They're my children."

There was a long pause. I could almost picture the captain's confused face—not unlike the face he'd given me when I told him I could read. He was clearly warring with whether or not to poll the people below decks to see if Judith and Nick were here.

His children were likely still enslaved, born of a union that could never truly be consensual—one of a white man and an enslaved woman. Those children had run to the Union Army for a reason. They wanted to be free.

"Don't do it," I said under my breath, willing Captain

Whitmore to hear me. "Don't tell him where to find them."

"If I could just come aboard and have a look—"

"Stay where you are, Mr. Donegall." The soldier's hand moved to his waist, hovering near his pistol. "We cannot allow you to molest anyone under the protection of this vessel."

"We do not know Nick or Judith," the captain's voice boomed. "I give you my word."

"All right, then." Mr. Edward Donegall sank back into his raft and picked up his oars. His lip quivered like he might protest, but he kept his mouth shut.

His eyes darted to the rest of the boat, scanning the portholes to look for his slaves. For a moment, his piercing gaze seemed to meet mine. I gasped and ducked under the window so that I could avoid eye contact. He may have been a father looking for his children, but he was also a slave owner looking for his lost property. He had no business being on this boat and searching the cabin.

He had no business owning people.

Donegall's boat teetered with the churning water as the gunboat picked up speed, leaving him to bob in its wake. Boots thudded against the aft staircase, and soon one of the Union soldiers was below deck.

"Captain Whitmore says you are at liberty to move about the ship."

"Thank you," I said. Then I nodded at my uncle. He sank to the floor and waved his hand at me, signaling that he was going to stay belowdecks to catch his breath.

I took the stairs two at a time, leaving the darkness of the chamber behind me as quickly as possible.

The sea breeze was a welcome greeting. I stood at the railing, watching the coastline float by. Just a few hours ago we'd been on one of those beaches, our feet tired, our thoughts frayed. We didn't know if the next person we ran into would be friend or foe. Now we were on our way to freedom.

On one of the deck benches behind me was a tattered copy of the same book Captain Whitmore had shoved in my hands.

The Ordnance Manual for the Use of the Officers of the United States Army.

I swiped it off the table and cracked it open. The Union Army had taken me in, had offered me protection—at least for the time being. I would do everything in my power to be of use to them. I'd make myself indispensable. So the first place I'd start was learning everything about them.

The wind whipped through Captain Whitmore's hair as our flotilla of longboats rowed out to St. Simons Island. He puffed up his chest, propping his foot up on the helm as his soldiers rowed us to shore. He cupped his hands over his eyes, shading his gaze from the westward sun as he scanned the nearing beach.

We landed at St. Simons Island on Gascoigne Bluff, or Gaston Bluff, as the Union soldiers called it. Captain Whitmore said it was one of the only places they could stow

gunboats, because it was a deep-water landing. Cotton plant-
ers from all over the island and surrounding counties used
this landing site to launch their goods to the open market. But
not anymore. This was Union territory now.

With a strategic point like this, the Union could resupply
their troops up and down the coast. More resources meant
that they could push farther inland. That was good news for
freeing more people in bondage. As plantations came under
fire, men, women, and children could use the commotion to
run to freedom—just as we had done.

We took the longboats to shore, leaving the gunboat
to float in the nearby deep water. It looked ominous on the
coastline, a waiting panther poised to pounce. I supposed
it provided us some protection just by being there. It might
scare off any Confederate soldiers looking to pick off a few
Union soldiers or discourage them from stealing a runaway
and putting them back in chains.

At least I hoped it would scare the Confederate soldiers.

There were several lean-to structures set up on the edge
of the beach and the bordering woodlands. A few yards back
from the beach were four squatty white cabins, and I knew
instantly what those were—slave quarters.

My heart rate ticked up. I was back on a plantation. But that
was where the similarities ended. There was no overseer and
no whipping post. And there were a lot of free people. There
had to be hundreds, more than I'd ever seen in the same place.

Where I grew up, free and enslaved people were not

allowed to congregate in large gatherings. The white folks got nervous that we'd all plan for freedom and revolt or run away. I remembered what had happened to my grandmother, when she was arrested at her church meeting. The guards had claimed they were planning freedom.

And now here were close to six hundred newly freed people. And none of the white people around them seemed bothered by their liberty. I was amazed.

"Well, here you are." Captain Whitmore raised his eyebrow at me and waved his hand with bravado. "St. Simons Island, as promised."

I nodded slowly, looking around me. My uncle stepped off first, sloshing through the water before holding his hand out to help me off the boat. My feet landed in the soft sand, and I turned and helped my cousins. When I turned back to the captain, he was already halfway across the beach, his eyes on a small group of uniformed men congregating on the grassy patch atop the bluffs.

"Wait," I said, struggling to keep up. This surely wasn't the end of our acquaintance. I didn't know where to settle my family or find food to fill our empty bellies. We still needed his assistance.

"Ahh!" Captain Whitmore stalked across the beach in the direction of the naval outpost tent in the shade. He brought his hand to his forehead in a salute. "Commodore Goldsborough, sir."

"Yes, yes." The commodore nodded, standing a little

straighter. He was clearly more senior than the captain, and he held his stature as the one in command. "Anything interesting to report?"

"We did run into a Mr. Donnegall on the water. He was looking for his lost slaves, Nick and Judith. Wondered if we might know their whereabouts." Captain Whitmore straightened his back, squaring his shoulders. "But we quickly dismissed him, and he was on his way soon after."

"Captain Whitmore, you should not have allowed him to return. You should have kept him. We don't know if he was a spy." The commodore shook his head, his cheeks reddening. "What other news have you?"

"We have rations to resupply." Captain Whitmore stood more at ease. My stomach gurgled at the mere mention of food rations, but I don't think he heard it. "And of course, more contraband——" His voice grew more distant as he and the commodore went for a promenade down the beach.

And that was it. We had been delivered to St. Simons Island as promised. But no lodgings or even a blanket were offered to us. I'm not sure what I had been expecting, but I expected at least a blanket.

And he'd called us *contraband*. There was that word again. I'd thought that after Captain Whitmore and I spoke on the boat, he would refer to me and my family as more than misplaced property. But apparently, I was wrong.

"They have a habit of doing that." A woman's voice sounded behind me.

"Doing what?" I asked.

"Disappearing." The woman flicked her head toward the company of men disappearing behind the bluff. When I turned my head back to her, she was unfastening a cap from a dented canteen. She held it out for me to take. "Here. It's fresh water, I know you need it."

"Thank you." I took it from her grasp. I was tempted to drink the whole thing—I was still *so* thirsty. But I passed it to my uncle instead. He had young mouths to take care of. And I guessed I could take care of myself for now.

"I'm Mary Shaw."

"Susie Baker. Good to meet you."

"There's more fresh water by the cabins. And I'll help you and your family rustle up something to eat. Don't worry. It's just us *contraband* on the island. And a few troops here and there."

"'Contraband,'" I said with a grumble. "I wish they wouldn't call us that."

"Well, that's what the Yankees call us." Mary rolled her eyes, cutting the Union soldiers a woeful glance. "Not exactly the title I was seeking either. I had my heart set on being called a free woman."

"So . . . we're not free?" I asked, following her to the cabins tucked away behind the tree line. I was beginning to feel nervous about my insistence on running into the arms of the Union Army. Maybe Mama was right—if we were going to run away from the farm, we should have headed north. At least in the North we might have been called free. But here . . . this was a strange sort of limbo in a pocket of the South that, until very recently, used to honor human bondage.

"We're not technically free. Not even the Union knows what to do with us. There's talk of a settlement, but you get all sorts of whispers on the island. There are always people coming in, bringing stories with them."

"But we're safe, right?"

She waited a moment to respond. She bowed her head, speaking softly. "Sometimes people disappear in the night. We suspect they're being snatched and dragged back to the plantation. So rule one is to stick close to the rest of the tents. Don't go thinking you can stake out a solitary plot in the woods."

I sank to the grass, looking out to the water. I was feeling unprotected and almost as lost as I had felt a couple days ago when we were running through the woods, escaping Grest Farm.

I scanned the trees and saw sassafras root growing in the brush. It was just where my mother had taught me to find it, and for a second I remembered my brother gathering it. I scrambled to my knees and dug my fingers in the dirt, unearthing the root cluster. I tore off a piece and then another, ripping it from the ground. And then I squirreled it away in my pocket.

My grandma would be proud, wherever she was right now.

Tonight I would boil some tea. I would have a taste of home. And then maybe I wouldn't feel so lost anymore.

* * *

Mary Shaw turned out to be a godsend. After only three days on the island, she had introduced me to almost everyone she knew at Gaston Bluff and at some of the neighboring camps. There were a number of settlements on this island of St. Simons, just like little villages, and we would go from one to the other on business, to call, or only for a walk. Lizzie Lancaster became a familiar and friendly face too, and she settled just down the road from us.

Back at the Bluff, I made myself useful in the best way I could. I helped with the washing. I was free—or as free as I could be. But freedom didn't offer me a job or money or land. Washing the officers' clothing was a way to earn money—fifty cents for cleaning a dozen pieces of clothing—but we had to provide the soap and starch.

I was boiling water for the laundry when a man cleared his throat behind me. When I turned, the officer that Captain Whitmore had saluted when we landed on the beach was standing right behind me. His bushy mustache bristled as he cleared his throat again.

"Oh, Commodore Goldsborough," I said, surprised to see him behind one of the cabins. The grass crunched beneath my boots as I took a step backward, and then another step and another until my back was flush against a tree. I was scared to be alone with him without anyone else present and wanted to put as much distance between us as possible.

He was the highest-ranking officer on the island. What could he want with me?

"Is there something I can help with?" I bowed my head, avoiding his curious eyes. "Perhaps some laundering?"

"Thank you, but I have other business with you," he said cordially. "Captain Whitmore spoke of you to me. I was pleased to hear of you being so capable. I wish you to take charge of a school for the children on the island."

"I will gladly do so." I beamed at him. This was an unexpected but very welcome surprise. My conversation with Captain Whitmore had been several days ago. I was beginning to think my offer of helping to teach the residents of St. Simons would go unanswered. I was ready and willing to serve my neighbors as the lead schoolteacher, but a school would take supplies I didn't have. My chalkboard and books were still at my grandmother's house in Savannah. I frowned, catching the commodore's attention. "If I could have some books, I could start a school."

"You shall have them." Commodore Goldsborough waved his arm dismissively, as if acquiring books wouldn't be a problem. There was a war going on, but he seemed confident in his supply lines. "It may take some weeks, but you will have enough books for your school." He raised his eyebrows and waved at a passing soldier. "Ahh, this is Chaplain French. Come all the way from Boston."

"Boston. That's quite far north. In Massachusetts, I believe." I lifted my face, looking at his sweaty brow and red-

dened cheeks. Suddenly I clammed up, unsure if I'd over-
reached. I bowed my head again, avoiding eye contact. "Good
to make your acquaintance, sir."

"You are a sharp one." The commodore pursed his lips,
clearly impressed by my knowledge of geography. They must
not have met many educated Black people, which was odd. I'd
thought there were more of us in the North. "Susie is going to
start a school for the little ones."

"And if you'd like, I can teach the older folks too." I offered
this, thinking about how curious my grandmother had been
as she leaned over my shoulder and watched me write passes
for her church meeting. She'd wanted to learn how to read
and write so badly. Young people were not the only people
who were eager to read.

"You sure you can take that on?" Chaplain French asked.

"Yes, sir. I've taught before."

"So a laundress and a teacher." Commodore Goldsborough
planted his hands on his hips and looked from me to the pile of
laundry and then back again. His eyes narrowed. It was as if he
was trying to figure me out. After a moment, he sighed and
looked to Chaplain French. "What an odd combination."

"Not to me, sir." I shook my head vigorously. I couldn't
think of anything more fitting for my skills—laundering
clothes was almost second nature to me. My grandmother
had taught me all she knew. And of course, I loved teaching.

It was a perfect match.

Chapter 9

WHILE I WAITED FOR MY BOOKS TO ARRIVE at St. Simons Island, I began the task of washing the regiment's uniforms.

And there were *a lot* of uniforms.

Each soldier received a shirt, a pair of underwear, one pair of wool socks, pants, and a wool coat. It was a meager allotment. The Union Army was under-resourced. And when the men arrived on the island, it seemed like every article of clothing was muddy or bloodied and in need of washing.

A mountain of dirty and worn jackets, muddy pants, and tattered white shirts sat piled on the beach near the cove. Every morning, I carried as much as I could to my laundry station behind the cabins and washed, dried, and pressed them. I was getting to know the uniforms pretty well—what a captain's uniform like Captain Whitmore's looked like, how to distinguish the filigree of a commodore from that of a colonel. I hadn't had the opportunity to encounter a general's uniform yet, but I suspected there weren't that many of them out there. You can't have too many people at the top.

No matter how much I laundered, this mound of clothing never seemed to disappear. It waxed and waned with the tides of soldiers who arrived every day, stopping by the island on their way elsewhere. Sometimes they would ferry back and forth from the gunboats in the deep water of the sea. But they never stayed long—a few days furlough, and then it was back to battling the Confederate troops.

This meant that I had to be efficient and expedient with my laundering.

I sat on a sturdy piece of driftwood by the beach. My hair was fastened in a scarf to protect my coils from the saltwater breeze whipping across the sound. I straddled a bucket of sudsy water and washed the officers' clothes while I monitored my boiling soap concoctions.

A vat of leftover lard and animal renderings bubbled in the cast-iron pot over an open flame. I stirred slowly, waiting for the fat to completely liquefy before adding in the lye and water. In a separate pot, I combined the lye-and-water mixture. I set this pot on the edge of the firepit, so that it would get hot but not too hot. Grandma always said that if you brought the lye to boil, you were going in the wrong direction.

She taught me well.

I lifted my head, looking out to the water as I wondered how my grandmother was doing. I liked to imagine her still in her tiny house in Savannah, humming a church hymn as she busied herself in the kitchen.

A young man knelt by the sea, swishing his jacket in the receding tide, like most men from the plantations did. They tried their best to rinse their clothing in the salt water, then slung them over driftwood to dry in the sun. But they never really got clean. For that you needed soap. Luckily, I knew how to make it.

"Can I assist you?" I called over to him and waved.

"It's all right, I guess. No need to trouble you." He bent down again, scowling at the stains on his shirt, then turned back at me with a sheepish smile.

"It's no trouble at all." I flicked my head toward the clotheslines behind me, each full with crisp and clean linens and clothing. "Yours won't be a burden. I'm almost finished with a new batch of soap. And I've got a few other girls helping me. The work will pass in no time."

"Well, you are pretty young to be leading your own brigade of women." He wagged a finger at me. "My name is Edward King, but my friends call me Ned."

"My name is Susie Baker, and I will call you by your given name." I blushed and looked away from him. "And I'm almost fourteen. And my grandmother says that's old enough to know better." I pursed my lips and sat up straighter. "Which means I gotta organize things around here that I can do—like making soap, maybe even teaching people to read and write. I can make a difference here."

"Is that right?" He chuckled as he stood from the water. "I don't have money to pay you, but I could do something for you in return. Say, collect firewood for you so you can keep boiling water and making soap. Or maybe build you something with my carpentry skills? Say the word and it's yours."

I smiled and nodded in thanks. I was about to ask him if he could build me a desk for my school, but Chaplain French called to me from across the beach.

"Ah, Susie." He kicked up sand as he hurried toward me. "Your books have just arrived from the North—two large boxes."

"Wonderful!" I bounced on the balls of my feet and clasped my hands. I turned to Edward. "Would you lend me a hand?"

We trudged through the sand to the commissary tent next to the officers' quarters. It was in the heart of their tent city. If there were streets in the maze of tents and firepits, it would be on Main Street. Chaplain French tapped one of the boxes with his boot.

"Some of them are straight from Boston. You know, that's where I'm from." He gripped the lapels of his jacket, smiling proudly. "There are testaments and novels and books of all sorts in here."

"This will do just nicely," I said as I sorted through the contents of the boxes. "Although I don't know where on God's green earth I'm going to put them."

I squinted down the row of tents bustling with activity

and saw a small cabin that sat back away from the tent city. This would be my schoolhouse. It wasn't big enough to hold too many people, but it was more private. But first we needed to get these boxes of books up to the new school.

I looked around for Edward, who was supposed to be doing the heavy lifting to the cabin. He had drifted over to a group of soldiers gathered around the central fire. They were all leaned over a folded piece of newspaper.

"What's that?" I asked.

"It's a proposed settlement of war for after the Union wins." Edward clenched his jaw, drawing his lips into a grim line. Whatever was on that page, he was not happy about it.

"May I?"

Edward handed me the paper, as if he no longer wanted to think about the words he just read.

"It says that upon Union victory, those Black persons on the Union side would remain free. Those in bondage are to work three days for their masters and three for themselves. Until such time as they are sent to Liberia. *Liberia?*"

"I don't know nothing about Liberia." Edward shoved his hands in his pockets, sneering sideways at the newspaper. "I'm from right here in Georgia. This is my home. I want to stay here as a free man."

"Liberia? As in West Africa?" I repeated it again, still unable to come to terms with it. I knew the South didn't want to share its land with newly freed people. But now it seemed that the North didn't want us either.

Chaplain French walked over. His eyes scanned the paper once and then another time. He let out a heavy sigh. "Would you rather go back to Savannah or go to Liberia?"

I thought to myself, *What do you think?* But I simply folded my arms, tilted my head, and reminded him that Savannah was my home, and it was where I intended to stay.

I thought President Lincoln was a Republican. Didn't he want to abolish slavery?

I knew what Mrs. Beasley would say—that I was over-simplifying things, that not all Republicans were abolitionists. *Stick to the facts at hand,* she'd say.

The president had withheld putting his full support behind freeing the enslaved, even after the start of the war. And now he wanted to send us out of the country, fearing that true equality could never be achieved here. He wanted to send us to Liberia, or Panama or Haiti. But my soil was right here. I raised my chin higher.

I was with Edward. This was our home.

"I doubt the Confederates will agree to this arrangement. At least that's the rumor flying around the troops. I wouldn't worry about it." Chaplain French carefully rolled up the newspaper and stuffed it in his back pocket, as if he could make the question of Liberian settlement disappear.

"Hmm," I mumbled under my breath, too frustrated to speak. Chaplain French didn't have to worry about being dragged off to bondage again or sent to a foreign country he knew nothing about. Peace of mind was the white man's privilege.

I didn't have that luxury.

"I wouldn't think any more on it. Truly."

I turned back to the commissary tent where my boxes of books still lay and motioned to Edward. "Let's get these boxes to the cabin. I have a school to make."

There weren't many permanent structures on the island and no proper schoolroom for miles. But I was used to conducting school in odd places. In Mrs. Woodhouse's kitchen, on my friend Katie O'Connor's porch, in my grandma's house with James Blouis. I thought back on my time at Mrs. Woodhouse's, when I'd corralled the early readers in the corner of her L-shaped kitchen and taught them their letters. This would be no different.

In the end, my schoolhouse was in the cabin and the yard surrounding it; our laps served as our desks. Of the six hundred residents on the island, most were women and children, which meant my classes were almost always large. During the day, after I worked as a laundress, I taught about forty children. And in the evenings, a number of adults came at night—all of them so eager to learn to read, to read above anything else.

Among my most regular adults was Edward King. I didn't know why he came so often. He already knew how to read. Still, he came dutifully most evenings, usually accompanied by his uncle, Charles O'Neal, and his best friend, Edward Davis, who we called Davis just to avoid confusion.

Chaplain French came to the school sometimes to lecture the pupils on his hometown of Boston and to tell us all tales of the North. When he wasn't otherwise engaged with his army duties, he helped some of the older students while I taught the little ones how to read.

"That's right—sound it out." I pointed to the word on the page, helping a younger boy. "*Ahhh—ahh—apple.* Good, that's good."

"Susie, what's going on?" The young boy turned his attention to the beach, where there seemed to be something of a commotion.

"Children, stay here." I rose slowly, taking in the scene unfolding in front of me. The men were mustering up, slinging their rifles over their shoulders and rushing across the beach. There were about ninety or so men. Edward King was among them, looking flustered.

"Edward," I called out. His frantic eyes met mine, and he rushed toward me. "What happened?"

"Adam Miller and Daniel Spaulding were chased by some Confederates just now, coming from Hope Place."

I nodded. Hope Place wasn't far from here. It lay between Gaston Bluff and the beach. So that meant that Confederate soldiers weren't far. A shot of adrenaline spiked my veins. I was scared. Charles O'Neal walked over to our little huddle. His shoulders were squared, and he stood about a head taller than most of the other men. He walked with the authority of their leader.

"Let's go." He peered at the tree line. "We think they're hiding in the woods. There's fallen logs and thick underbrush there. That's where they'll be."

He ran in the direction of the woods, the perfect cover for enemy soldiers lying in wait. My chest tightened. As I watched Edward run toward the tree line, his boots kicking up sand as he disappeared behind the bluffs, my throat seized like I was about to cry. I had seen a few skirmishes since leaving the farm, but I hadn't cried since I left my grandmother in Savannah and my parents and siblings on Grest Farm. Watching Edward leave was like parting with family. And it didn't sit well with me.

I knew in that moment that I couldn't lose him.

I resolved to roll my sleeves up and do everything in my power to help him and the rest of the boys fighting. I looked around the beach. There was much work to be done.

We were not safe here. The Union Army wasn't protecting us. They mostly floated offshore in their gunboats, relatively removed from the goings-on of the camp. The few soldiers that remained on the island were otherwise engaged in keeping Union Army supply lines open. Sure, their mighty ships were a deterrent, but obviously that wasn't foolproof. There were chinks in our armor. And Confederates had found their way into our safehold.

The rebels could sneak past the gunboats under the cover of night and get on the island to capture anyone venturing out alone and carry them to the mainland. It was up to us to try to create a safe space.

"Hey, you over there!" I yelled to one of the younger men near the makeshift dock on the beach. "Take a boat as fast you can and tell the marines out on them gunboats that we need their assistance. As many men as they can spare. Go quickly!"

We began reassembling our tents around a fire. Since the Confederates had not yet been found, it was best we stayed closer to each other.

Mary Shaw plopped down next to me with a huff. She leaned back and rolled her neck from side to side, trying to loosen her tight muscles.

"Did you get the watch parties set up?" I asked.

"Yes. We got guards around the clock." She yawned. "I'm sorry."

"Don't apologize." I sat on the ground next to her and grabbed her hand. "You didn't sleep a wink last night."

"Neither did you." She shrugged.

She was right. With most of the men searching for the rogue Confederates, every sound scared me. I couldn't sleep all night, and tonight wouldn't be any different.

The sound of crunching gravel made me jump. There, coming down the path, were the men who'd run off to search for the Confederates. Edward was among them, and the day's skirmish was fresh in his sad eyes. He hung back, wringing his hat in his hands. I heaved myself upward and wove through the returning watchmen until I got to my friend.

"What's wrong?" I looked over his shoulder, searching for another familiar face, but I didn't see anyone else coming down the road. "Where is your uncle Charles?"

"We searched the woods, and Uncle Charles was right. The Confederates were right where he suspected—hiding in the woods behind a large log, in thick underbrush. My uncle was the first to see them, but . . . he's not coming back to camp."

"No!" I clasped my hands over my mouth, utterly shocked at the news of Charles O'Neal's death.

"John Brown was also killed." Edward sniffled into his sleeve. "We couldn't even find their bodies. Everything was happening so fast. And John Baker was shot too."

"There he is," I said, pointing to the lagging group of watchmen coming up the lane. Two men were carrying John Baker, shouldering his weight on each of their arms. I sucked in a sharp breath. "He's in really bad shape."

"At least he still might live." Edward's voice quivered, and he looked away from me. "I have no one left. My uncle was the only family I had anywhere near us. I'm alone."

"You're not alone." I grabbed his hand, interlocking my fingers with his. "And you have family. In me."

"What are you saying?" His eyes brightened slightly.

"Well." I looked out to sea and then back again at his dark brown eyes. "You and me, we can find home with each other."

"We need help over here! Fresh rags!" the doctor yelled to no one in particular. He spotted me standing a few yards away and waved frantically at me. "Laundress, your assistance, please!"

"I have to go, but I'll see you soon." I squeezed Edward's hands one last time before releasing them.

John Baker was in a terribly bad state, bloodied and bruised. His hands, which were crossed over his chest, trembled every now and then.

I grabbed a bag of supplies from my laundry station, then sprinted to the doctor as fast as I could. John Baker was near death. If he didn't get help now, he would surely die.

"Thank goodness." The doctor grabbed a wad of clean towels and laid them over the bullet wound on Baker's leg. "Keep them coming. Boil some water, please."

"The others?" John Baker asked quietly. "John Brown? And Charles?"

"I'm sorry, sir." I shook my head, and he understood what I meant.

"Maybe they didn't have food. I survived by laying quiet and eating wild grapes."

"Okay, grab his leg and put pressure on it." The doctor ripped one of the clean towels in half and then split that piece into a thinner strand. "I need to tie this around his thigh to stop the bleeding. It slows the circulation to this part of the body."

"Doc, we've got another one."

"Coming. Susie, you handle this one while I tend to the other one."

I stared at him, wide-eyed with panic. Handle it? I wasn't sure I could handle it, but for some reason I nodded. "Okay. I'll nurse him."

I dipped a washrag in a bucket of water, then brought it to his brow, wiping the sweat and blood away from the face. I hoped it would bring him comfort.

Suddenly, John Baker curled into a ball and howled in pain. I dropped the towel on the ground and searched his side, trying to find the source of the pain. I finally found another gunshot wound festering in the flesh.

I pressed it with my hand, just as I'd seen the doctor do. But the blood kept coming out.

"Help." My voice croaked as I waved my arms at the doctor. But he was tending to the other patient. I lowered my arms and turned my hands over. My eyes grew wide as I stared at my bloody palms.

Chapter 10

I GRIPPED MY KNEES TO MY CHEST, ROCKING back and forth as I looked down into the sand, trying to catch my breath. My bloody hands trembled against my kneecaps. I had seen carnage. I was barely fourteen.

There was suddenly much activity on the island. The troops, who finally had arrived, expertly canvassed the area in their search for our intruders. Patrols ran through the perimeter of our tent city, and behind that they searched the scattered outbuildings and crude shelters spotted across the island. It was only a matter of time before they found the culprits.

I stood up. Sitting around was a luxury I didn't have. I needed to be useful.

I went to the medic tent, where John Baker now slept in fits and starts. There didn't seem to be much use for me at his side, so I fetched a bucket of water and poured it in the pot. The doctor had asked me to keep water boiling at all times, so that was what I would focus on—boiling water and clean strips of cloth. I didn't want to be caught off guard again. I worked on preparing for the next disaster.

Because there would be another disaster. That was our life on St. Simons Island.

"Excuse me. You're not injured, are you?" a tall soldier inquired. He had a kind face with thick eyebrows and earnest eyes. It seemed like he was genuinely concerned. "Hello there, are you hurt?"

"It's not mine." I gulped down a wave of bile rising in my throat. I was woozy and nauseous at the sight of my hands, which were still stained with blood. The red had dried and dulled a bit in the sea breeze, but it was still there. "I'll return to the patients momentarily. I just needed to get some air."

"That's good to hear. You must be one of our nurses. I'm Captain Trowbridge."

"I'm Susie Baker."

"I've heard of you—from the commodore." His earnest eyes lit up with curiosity. "You're the schoolteacher and laundress, yes?"

"Yes, sir."

"And I suppose now we can add 'nurse' to your list of manifold accomplishments." He tipped his hat and then cleared his throat. "Are you all right? You look a bit peaked."

"Okay, I guess." I shrugged. "Will you and your men stay on the island this time? We need your protections, sir."

"I'll leave as many soldiers as I can spare. But that might not be many. There is a war going on."

"Sir!" A winded soldier yelled from across the beach. He and three other soldiers carried a wooden boat over their shoulders. Their boots kicked up sand as they marched over to where the captain and I were standing. They set the boat at Trowbridge's feet.

"What's this?" Captain Trowbridge pointed at the small boat between us.

"We found the Confederate boat." The soldier wiped his brow with his sleeve. "Just in the cove near the old plantation quarters."

I gasped. That was not far from where I slept—right where my buckets for laundry were. I wrapped my arms around my chest, trying to hold myself together. I thought I had carved out a safe life on this island—as safe as it could be in the midst of war. But this hit too close to home. If I had been awake at the crack of dawn when the Confederate soldiers were milling about, I could have been snatched up and taken back to the Grest plantation.

My freedom was a thin sliver of truth, very fragile, and it could be broken at any moment.

"Those men can't be far." Trowbridge ran his fingers through his hair as he looked to the Gaston Bluff settlement just behind the tree line. "I suspect someone is helping them hide."

"Never." I shook my head, looking to Mary Shaw for her to corroborate. But as she looked at me, she shook her head.

"You'd be surprised how hard it is for some folks to change." She sighed heavily. "Some people don't know how to turn their backs on the plantation and its ways. It's got ahold of their minds."

"The Confederates can't leave the island on this boat now that we have it," the captain said to the soldiers. "Search the island again. And check and see if there's been any suspicious activity. Any boats go missing? Are all the wagons accounted for? Has anyone noticed a contraband absent? All of these are pertinent questions."

He marched off in the direction of the road, his men following closely at his heels. I was conflicted in my heart. White men marching through our homes and settlements looking for collaborators. My gut instinct said they couldn't be trusted. White men ransacking our quarters—it was like another day on the plantation.

But there might be traitors in our midst. And they were harboring Confederate soldiers. Confederate soldiers who had killed Edward King's uncle and countless others. That person was putting all of us in danger.

After I came to that grim realization, I did not protest the officers' search anymore.

The flap to Mary's tent opened quickly, startling Edward and me from our perch near the small stove. Her eyes were wide, her breathing coming fast and quick.

"They found him!" She waved her hand quickly. "They found the man harboring the Confederates. Come quick."

"You should rest. Let the other men take care of this." I gripped Edward's shoulder. He had been out with his troop all day and had only just got off his feet. But he grabbed his rifle from the table in the middle of the room and slung it over his shoulder. He'd been carrying it around ever since he'd picked it off of a rebel's body in one of the many skirmishes around the island.

"I have to see this through." He clenched his jaw. "My uncle . . ."

His throat quivered as he struggled to complete his sentence. Then he held his hand out. It was an invitation for me to join him on the journey to the culprit's house.

"All right, then." Mary nodded to the both of us and moved quickly down the path. Her skirts brushed against the well in the middle of the quad as she made a hard right turn.

Just down the road, more inland on the island, was Mr. Hazzard's old plantation. The place was smaller than the settlement at the Bluff, and it looked mostly abandoned. But I knew who lived here—an old man named Henry Capers.

"I don't believe it," I mumbled under my breath. He'd always been cordial, albeit quiet. He kept mostly to himself. We only saw him every now and then when he cut grass for his horse and transported it back to his home on a boat. Mr.

Hazzard had long since fled. He'd left Henry behind because he was an elderly enslaved man and not of much value to him on the run.

"Come out, Mr. Capers!" Captain Trowbridge boomed from outside his home.

"You've already searched the cabin." Henry Capers stepped out with his head hanging low. He gripped his hat and took it off. "There's no one in there, sir. It's just me."

"There's no one else in there *today*. But I suspect there were more people hiding in your loft until quite recently." Trowbridge stroked his beard, peering into the old house's windows. "You asked the commanding officer on duty to borrow a boat, is that correct?"

"Yes, sir." The old man bobbed his head in agreement. "I cut grass to feed my horses. And I row it back to the farm there."

"So where's the boat?"

"Sir?" Mr. Capers shifted nervously on his feet.

"You were supposed to return the boat. You did not return it."

"I—"

"We should burn the whole thing down." An officer behind Trowbridge waved a torch. There were shouts of agreement in the ranks.

"No, sir!" Mr. Capers stepped forward, clasping his hands together as if in prayer. He pleaded with Trowbridge. "Sir!"

"Say it plainly, Mr. Capers, and no one will burn down

the cabin." Trowbridge put his hand over his heart and nodded encouragingly. "Did you provide shelter to Confederate soldiers?"

"Yes, but . . . but only for a night. They forced my hand, sir. They threatened to kill me if I didn't help them. What was I supposed to do?"

"You know those men killed several men on the island? They came here intent on wreaking havoc, killing more, possibly stealing some of you away."

"Well, I—"

"Let it be known that to harbor Confederate soldiers on this island is unacceptable behavior. I will not tolerate it!" Captain Trowbridge turned away from the old man and faced the crowd. His jaw was tight, his expression severe. "You are either with us or against us. Is that understood?"

"I am sorry, sir," Mr. Capers sobbed, but Captain Trowbridge still had his back turned toward him. He was most interested in addressing the gathering crowd.

"The punishment for aiding the enemy will be swift and severe."

"Please do not burn my home."

"Your home will not be burned," the captain said as he turned to face Mr. Capers again. "I already gave you that assurance, and I am a man of my word. But you will not be allowed to stay here."

"What?" Mr. Capers balked.

"I cannot trust that you will not jeopardize my troops or

these people who are under my protection. You will go from this place at once—back to the mainland."

"Oh Lord," Mary Shaw whispered. Her hand flew up to her face. "He can't go back to the mainland. He'll be captured for sure."

"He wanted to be with the Confederates so bad," Edward said. "He can go be with them."

Then he stalked off toward the road, gripping his gun so tightly that his knuckles went pink. Sending Mr. Capers back to the mainland wasn't going to bring his uncle Charles back.

Chapter 11

I GAVE EDWARD HIS SPACE. HE NEEDED IT. AFTER losing his uncle, he had withdrawn from the world.

I busied myself with picking berries. The island had patches of blackberries that grew wild, but the brambles closer to camp had been picked dry. The ones farther inland were ripe for the taking.

I loved the taste of a juicy berry, but these weren't just for my enjoyment. These were for pie filling that Mary was going to make. I'd make the dough with the flour rations I'd been saving. We'd make pies to sell to the Union troops, who were always coming and going on the island. And they were always looking for a taste of home—something homemade like their mamas used to make.

We needed the money. Despite all the work we did for the Union—washing clothes and teaching at the school—we were not being paid for our services. I was grateful just to be on the island, enjoying my semi-freedom. But I needed to save up money.

One day I would buy a house just like Mrs. Woodhouse's or Mrs. Beasley's. And I would run a school out of it. It was my dream.

A shot fired through the air. I gasped, feeling my heart rate flutter. It took me a moment to gather my thoughts, but once I did, I realized the shots were coming from a distance. I hoped it wasn't another Confederate soldier. It had been days since the last Confederates were here on the island. We didn't need any more.

But since then, the men had organized pickets around the island, and they were manned all hours of the day. It was highly unlikely there was an enemy shooting in the breeze. Whoever was in these woods was a fellow comrade.

"Don't shoot," I yelled out. "I'm unarmed."

"Susie?" a familiar voice belted through the trees. It was unmistakably Edward. "What are you doing all the way out here?"

"I'm picking berries for pies. You know the best ones are farther from the settlement. What are *you* doing out here?"

It had been a few days since I'd seen him. And I was a bit miffed about that. But I understood.

"Target practice." Edward shrugged sheepishly as he rubbed the back of his neck. He pointed to a row of rotten apples that stood on an old fence a dozen yards away.

"You can shoot all the way over there? And that accurately?" My eyebrows shot up.

"Well, sometimes. I'm not great with guns yet."

"How could you be? They didn't let us carry them before."

"I know. But now we have guns. And I intend to use mine. I'm never going to be caught unaware like that again."

"You know it wasn't your fault, right? Uncle Charles knew the risks running after those Confederates."

"It's not about fault. It's about being prepared. From here on out, I'll be prepared."

He lifted his gun and pointed it at that row of rotten apples. He eased the butt of his gun closer to his chest and squinted toward the target. His finger quivered on the trigger for a moment until he finally pressed it. The shot echoed through the woods, followed by the unmistakable sound of a bullet piercing the core of an apple.

"Oh!" I clasped my hands together and bounced on the balls of my feet. "You got one!"

"You might just be my good-luck charm."

"Okay, now let me try." I held an expectant hand out between us, wiggling my fingers at the gun.

"You can't shoot a gun," Edward scoffed, shaking his head.

"Well, you couldn't shoot one either, until you taught yourself. Now come on. I've got to learn this too. Those Confederate soldiers landed right near my laundry."

"I didn't think of that." His smirk faded.

"Me neither. Now it's the only thing I can think about. Will you teach me?"

"All right, then." He reloaded the rifle with gunpowder. When he finished, he flipped the gun handle toward me.

The butt of the rifle was smooth and cold, and it weighed about ten pounds. Just looking at it scared me. This gun had the power to kill a person. It could tear through wood and metal, could rip through flesh. I held it in my hands for a moment, breathing steadily as I took in the responsibility. Then I gave Edward a solemn nod. I was ready to begin training.

"Hold it up like I did. May I?" Edward walked around me, shifting my stance with his patient hands. "Bring it lower. You don't want it to clip your chin. When you pull the trigger, there's some kickback. You'll want to brace for that."

"Okay," I said, digging my heels deeper into the dirt.

"Also, never point the tip of the gun at a friendly. And use the notch at the top of the barrel to guide your shot. Okay, if you're ready—"

I put pressure on the trigger, and the bullet ripped out of the gun.

"Whoa!" I gave a breathy, nervous laugh. I squinted toward the apples. "Did I get one? I don't think I got one."

"Definitely not. We're going to have to work on this."

It was a good thing Edward was helping me learn how to shoot. I knew from my experience teaching other people that you reinforce your own learning in the process. So technically I was helping him out too.

And that was something I could live with.

I raised the rifle to my chest again and aimed at the line of apples on the fence post.

"You are quite a woman," Edward said. "Did you really mean what you said the other day? That we're family?"

I lowered the gun. "Of course I did."

"Then let's make it official. Let's get married."

My grandmother always said I was old enough to know better. And I knew better than to pass this opportunity by.

"Yes. I'll marry you."

"All right, class." I closed my copy of *The Biblical Reader*, which Chaplain French had given me for our advanced elocution studies. It wasn't my students' favorite part of school—they preferred taller tales than these selected Bible verses could provide—but the book was similar to what I'd used to learn to read: my treasured, tattered Bible from James Blouis, the landlord's son. I sagged against the rickety table, surveying my classroom, which had already devolved into loud chitchat and games. I tapped the spine of the book against the desk, and the knocking noise seemed to regain their attention. "I think we've had enough of this, hmm? That's it for the day."

A few of the smaller children ran out the door immediately, kicking up sand as they went to go play, as if they couldn't be done with my lecture on inflection and modulation soon enough. I wasn't offended. One day they'd appreciate all the letters and words they had rattling around in their heads. For now, they could be children and run around in the late summer sun. A few of the girls hung back, giggling under their breaths. One raised her hand.

"Ms. Susie?" she asked, breaking into a toothy grin. "Is it true you got married over the weekend?"

"Yes, I did." I blushed, turning away from my students' eager eyes. The ceremony had been small, with only a few witnesses, followed by a simple supper that evening. I didn't want to make a big fuss about it, especially with the war still raging on. But I was quite happy to be married to Edward King. "I suppose it's about time y'all started calling me Mrs. King. Do tell the others."

"*Mrs. King!*" one of the girls squealed, sending the group tumbling into a fit of excited laughter. Only one of the girls appeared to be distracted from all the wedding talk. She peered through the doorway and spotted a fleet of rafts coming onto shore. It wasn't an uncommon sight——gunboats often moored in the deep waters near the bluff and furloughed their soldiers while they resupplied.

"What are they doing over there?" She pointed to the tree line, where soldiers were unloading large trunks and stacking them on the sand.

"That's a good question." I said as I watched the flurry of supply boxes being deposited on the ground. "Never you mind, girls. Those soldiers will do what they do. And we'll do what we need to do. And I'm sure that means chores need to be completed."

The children scampered off, scattering across the beach

and through the tall grass, running in the opposite direction as the tents, cabins, and cookhouse, where their mothers undoubtedly waited for them to help with daily chores. But I was heartened that most of them still had a playful side. Children were remarkably resilient, even in wartime.

It reminded me of my time with my siblings in Savannah. A war was brewing around us, and we were still technically in bondage, but we found a way to play together anyway. I wondered if they still had a chance to play.

"May I intrude?" a familiar voice asked.

"Oh, Captain Trowbridge." I looked over my shoulder. "It's no intrusion at all."

"I heard a bit about your lesson." He dipped his head lower, trying to look me in the eyes. He was the only white man who ever tried to do that. I found it unnerving. He soon gave up and stood straighter, looking over my shoulder at my copy of *The Biblical Reader*. He chuckled under his breath. "Don't you think the children are a little young to speak of Exodus and plagues and bondage?"

"Respectfully, sir—no, I do not. In a way, these children have lived it." I lifted my head and met his gaze, hoping he could see the stories of Exodus and bondage mirrored in my eyes. Instead of being reproached for my impertinence, the captain nodded in agreement.

"Quite right. That is a point well made, Ms. Baker."

"Actually, sir," I said, dipping my head low again and trailing off. I'd already been so bold; I didn't know if I could push it slightly further. But I felt compelled to tell him my preferred name. "It's Mrs. King now."

"Oh, congratulations are in order, then." He smiled, then looked at me. "And judging by the way most of the adults are reading around the Bluff, I gather I should trust your judgment as an educator."

"Thank you, sir. My husband, Edward King, helps me teach when he doesn't have watch duties. He has a way with some of the older folks." I relaxed my shoulders a bit. Then I gestured to the tables being set up on the beach and the trunks being ferried back and forth from the gunboat. "What is going on over there?"

"Those are registration tables." His nostrils flared as he smiled proudly. "We're going to have sign-ups to fill the rest of General Hunter's regiment."

"You mean, we can officially fight for the Union?" Black men had not been allowed to join the ranks of the army. It was peculiar—the Union was fighting against the slaveholders of the South, but it wouldn't let the formerly enslaved fight alongside them. I'd always found that strange and shortsighted.

"The men of course are welcome to our ranks. It should have happened long ago, but now news of the island's skirmish with the rebels has reached General Hunter. He's impressed with the bravery shown by the men on the island. He's instructed me and my brother and Lieutenant Walker to find men to fill his regiment."

"That's good. The boys are already fending off

Confederates. Might as well make it official and get paid to do so."

"Ehhh, yes." He hesitated and blinked. I wondered why his otherwise honest eyes seemed guarded. "General Hunter has sanctioned this registration for a Black regiment, and we now know that the federal government will sanction it."

"I would like to be the first to sign up to help." I squared my shoulders and stepped forward. "I can shoot just about as good as any man here. I hit my targets most times."

"Really?" He stroked his chin as he appraised me anew. "That is very impressive."

"And I know how to make soap. I laundered almost every uniform out there."

"Well, all right then, Mrs. King. We shall enroll you as a laundress." He clapped his hands together as if it was a done deal. "See? The regiment's taking shape. Which is a good thing too, given that training needs to commence immediately. We'll likely only have a few months to get the men in shape before we ship out."

"Ship out, sir?" My voice croaked. I had been so focused on joining the Union fight, I didn't even think about leaving the bluff. It was the latter part of August 1862, and in less than five months, I'd managed to make a life on the island. Even though life was difficult, I was nervous to leave. It was familiar. But perhaps our next location would be better and more secure?

"I'm afraid we will have to leave this post eventually."

He sighed, wistfully gazing across the beach as the seagulls flocked at low tide. "But we can make a difference in this war. I know it. We just have to join the fray."

With the regiment filled, the brave men from the Sea Islands were called the First South Carolina Volunteer Infantry Regiment. It was one of the first Union regiments to be completely comprised of Black men, and most of them had been held in bondage. I had a number of relatives in Company E of this regiment—several uncles, some cousins, a husband—and a number of cousins in other companies. They were willing to dedicate their lives to ensure a Union victory.

I hoped the Union would properly reward their efforts.

Chapter 12

CAPTAIN TROWBRIDGE DIDN'T LEAVE US LIKE the other officers had. He stayed on the island, training our brave boys, helping us change them from men into soldiers. Just as I held daily classes on reading and arithmetic, Trowbridge held daily instruction in shooting and scouting. These were all things that would help our regiment when we went on the move.

By October 1862, we were ordered to evacuate the island and move out to the front—just as Captain Trowbridge had predicted. The entire regiment boarded the *Ben-De-Ford*, a transport vessel bound for Beaufort, South Carolina. It was cramped, but we managed to make it work. Edward and I squeezed past our fellow soldiers as we made our way to the top deck, where we found Davis.

"I'm not going to miss Gaston Bluff." I stared over the

railing, watching St. Simons Island grow smaller on the horizon. "Life there has been hard."

Edward nodded quietly beside me, then turned his attention to his uniform.

"It's not what I was expecting." He tugged at the red cloth
of his coat. His eyes narrowed as he looked at one of the white
officers clad in the Union's classic blue uniform. "It's embar-
rassing."

"It's really not that bad." I tilted my head to the side, trying to see the better angle of things. It was a uniform. And red
or not, Edward looked quite dashing in it.

"If you ask me, it's dangerous." Davis unbuttoned his
jacket and shrugged out of it. It hung limply in his hands as he
said, "The rebels will see us miles away."

"He has a point." Edward eyed me from the corner of his
eyes. His bottom lip jutted out in a pout.

"I'm sure we'll be able to scrounge up some other uniforms when we reach Beaufort." I nodded confidently. We
were leaving the small-town life of Gaston Bluff for the bigger
city of Beaufort. There were going to be shops there, more
people, opportunity. "We can buy supplies in town with the
money we get from signing up."

"I haven't gotten anything yet." Davis nudged Edward
with his elbow. "What about you?"

"No." Edward shook his head. "They told us to ask about
it later."

"They told me the same thing." I looked around the deck

and saw Captain Trowbridge walking to the bow of the boat. "Captain Trowbridge, a word?"

"Yes, but I only have a moment." He looked at his pocket watch and raised his eyebrow at the time. "We'll be in Beaufort soon. And then on to Camp Saxton."

"Sir, we were wondering about our uniforms."

"And pay," Davis added, smiling uncomfortably.

"Your uniforms can be sorted out when we get to the old fort."

"And our pay?" Edward asked.

"Well . . ." Captain Trowbridge's voice trailed off as he struggled to find what to say. "Rest assured, you boys will be well taken care of. There is a commissary on the base, which will provide you with what you need."

"Are you saying we won't be getting paid?"

"I'm not saying that." He looked off into the distance, as if he was trying to steer the conversation into a more favorable direction.

"There's that look again." My eyes tightened as I studied his facial expression. "You made that same face a few weeks ago when you first mentioned enlisting in the regiment. I asked you about pay then, and you hesitated."

"As astute as ever, Ms. Baker." He breathed in deeply, half impressed, half annoyed.

"Actually, sir, it's Mrs. King now, remember?"

"Oh yes, I'm sorry I forgot. Please accept my hearty congratulations."

"Thank you, sir." Edward gave a tight smile, which waned after a few moments. "May we please discuss the wages? Me being married now, that sort of thing is important to a family."

"There is a bit of a backlog with the federal government right now. And we have no money in the coffers. But I am making sure that commissary will provide you and your families with provisions."

"Are the other soldiers going without pay?"

"Well . . ." The captain shrugged apologetically.

"That's what I thought," Edward grumbled under his breath. He'd known the answer before he'd even asked it— only the Colored Troops were suffering the indignities of service without pay. The white soldiers didn't have to worry about that. Not worrying was their privilege.

For now, we were completely dependent on the scraps offered by the Union Army.

When we arrived in Beaufort, Captain Trowbridge and the men he had enlisted went to camp at Old Fort, which they named Camp Saxton. I stayed behind with the other wives and children. The families of the Black soldiers had to depend wholly on what they received from the commissary established by General Saxton. Many members of Company E had large families, and as they received no wages, their wives were forced to support themselves and children by washing for the officers and soldiers of the gunboats and by making cakes and pies, which they sold to the boys in camp.

I had many responsibilities juggling the laundering and the pie baking. Since our husbands were still not getting paid for their work, there was no hope that us women would be paid for our assistance to the regiment.

We had to step up our laundry enterprise. That meant banding together and helping share the workload so that we could handle as many customers as possible. I had help from Mary Shaw and Lizzie Lancaster most days, so that passed the time.

Mary's deep timbre belted:

Oooh, the sun going down,
And I won't be here long.
Oooh, the sun going down,
And I won't be here long.
Oooh, then I be going home.
Oooh, I can't let this dark cloud catch me here.
Oooh, I can't stay here long,
Oooh, I be at home.

"My back is hurting something fierce," Mary said during a lull in the singing. She stood up and gripped her sides, swaying back and forth. She looked so amusing, I couldn't help but laugh. "What's so funny?"

"Nothing?" I stifled my laughter as I wrung out another shirt. "It's just that you remind me of my grandmother. She used to do something similar when she ran her laundry."

"Well, I feel as old as a grandmother. I wouldn't feel so worn out if the army would just pay the men."

I chuckled mirthlessly. The men had gone several months already without pay.

"There's a rumor that the government might decide to give them half pay." I shook my head. "It's not right."

"Half pay! That's an insult! Should they only fight half the time?"

"Full pay or nothing. That's what Edward says." I sighed heavily, rolling up my sleeves to continue my washing. But I was distracted by all the hammering going on around me. Some men were in the middle of the square in Beaufort, constructing a small wooden stage. I looked on wistfully. "Do you think the government will ever see fit to paying *us*?"

There was a moment of silence while the women pondered this. We'd been so in a huff about the men not getting paid that I don't think any of us stopped to think about what our contribution was worth. But we were the glue holding the camp together, keeping the men clean and fed and tending to the wounded. In this new world we were building, what was a woman's worth?

What was our worth?

"I can't think straight with all this racket going on." Mary pointed to the stage being constructed in the square. It was an artful dodge from the probing question I'd raised. "What do you think it's for? You think this is all for Christmas?"

"Edward said it was something to do with a presidential

announcement." I gritted my teeth as I plunged my hands into the sudsy water. "I hope it's not about the settlements after the war. I'm not going to Liberia."

"This is our home. And we're fighting for it. The least we can do is choose where we want to live. Same as any white man."

The president had gone back and forth on what to do about slavery.

"Mmmhmm. Let's see what this Lincoln's gotta say now."

Chapter 13

AWEEK AFTER CHRISTMAS, WORD OF President Lincoln's proclamation had spread through the camp. By January 1, 1863, we were all atwitter about what the executive order contained. Would the president stick to his earlier announcement that he intended to free enslaved people and hold enslavers in open rebellion?

I gathered in the square alongside my husband, Mary Shaw, and Edward Davis. I wrapped my shawl around me, fighting off the bitter cold that had swept through the city after Christmas. On the dais was a presentation of two beautiful flags, one from a lady in Connecticut and the other from Reverend Cheever.

After the presentation, Chaplain French stepped up to the pulpit to introduce the document that we'd all been waiting for.

"It is fitting that this proclamation be read by one of the

preeminent figures of this city, Dr. W. H. Brisbane." Chaplain French held his hand over his heart and nodded. Then he stepped aside to make room for Dr. Brisbane to take center stage.

"Ladies and gentlemen, the time has come for us to hear the words we've been waiting to hear for a long time. I will read the president's transcription verbatim. This is what our president has proclaimed for the whole country to hear:

"January 1, 1863
"A Transcription
"By the President of the United States of America:
"A Proclamation.
"Whereas, on the twenty-second day of September, in the year of our Lord one thousand eight hundred and sixty-two, a proclamation was issued by the President of the United States, containing, among other things, the following, to wit:

"That on the first day of January, in the year of our Lord one thousand eight hundred and sixty-three, all persons held as slaves within any State or designated part of a State, the people whereof shall then be in rebellion against the United States, shall be

then, thenceforward, and forever free; and
the Executive Government of the United
States, including the military and naval
authority thereof, will recognize and maintain
the freedom of such persons, and will do no
act or acts to repress such persons, or any of
them, in any efforts they may make for their
actual freedom.

"That the Executive will, on the first
day of January aforesaid, by proclamation,
designate the States and parts of States,
if any, in which the people thereof,
respectively, shall then be in rebellion
against the United States; and the fact
that any State, or the people thereof, shall
on that day be, in good faith, represented
in the Congress of the United States by
members chosen thereto at elections wherein
a majority of the qualified voters of such
State shall have participated, shall, in the
absence of strong countervailing testimony,
be deemed conclusive evidence that such
State, and the people thereof, are not then in
rebellion against the United States.

"Now, therefore I, Abraham Lincoln,
President of the United States, by virtue of
the power in me vested as Commander-in-

Chief, of the Army and Navy of the United
States in time of actual armed rebellion
against the authority and government of the
United States, and as a fit and necessary
war measure for suppressing said rebellion,
do, on this first day of January, in the year
of our Lord one thousand eight hundred
and sixty-three, and in accordance with my
purpose so to do publicly proclaimed for
the full period of one hundred days, from
the day first above mentioned, order and
designate as the States and parts of States
wherein the people thereof respectively,
are this day in rebellion against the United
States, the following, to wit…"

I listened intently to the list of states still in open rebellion,
praying for Georgia to be named. Dr. Brisbane rattled through
a litany of states—"Arkansas, Texas, Louisiana, (except the
Parishes of St. Bernard, Plaquemines, Jefferson, St. John,
St. Charles, St. James Ascension, Assumption, Terrebonne,
Lafourche, St. Mary, St. Martin, and Orleans, including the
City of New Orleans) Mississippi, Alabama"—my goodness,
the list went on and on.

Finally he said, "Georgia."

I gripped onto Edward's sleeve, pulling him closer to me.

"Did you hear that?" I yanked on his sleeve harder until

he was at just the right height for our foreheads to touch. We
stood there for a while, the crowd cheering around us. The
jubilation brought tears even to Edward's eyes. And I didn't
blame him—I was crying too.

We were finally free.

And for the first time in a long time, I felt seen and maybe
even a little understood. It was as if President Lincoln was
looking at me, saying, "You are free."

Dr. Brisbane read on,

> "And by virtue of the power, and for the
> purpose aforesaid, I do order and declare
> that all persons held as slaves within said
> designated States, and parts of States, are,
> and henceforward shall be free; and that the
> Executive government of the United States,
> including the military and naval authorities
> thereof, will recognize and maintain the
> freedom of said persons."

Of course, the proclamation only freed people in states
that were in open rebellion. That nuance was not lost on me.
This was not a free ticket for everyone in bondage, and it
clouded my own happiness.

> "And I further declare and make known,
> that such persons of suitable condition, will

be received into the armed service of the
United States to garrison forts, positions,
stations, and other places, and to man
vessels of all sorts in said service...."

"Now that the federal government officially recognizes
the Black regiments, you think that means we'll finally get
paid?" Edward pulled away from me, gripping my shoulders
as he smiled slyly.

"Let's just enjoy this moment, okay?" I said, still doubting
the federal government. We would soon see whether or not
they'd make good on their promises.

The fiddler struck his strings while the banjo player plucked
along in harmony. The evening sky filled with smoke as a roast
ox turned on a spit in the middle of the square. For many of
us, it had been a while since we'd smelled meat, let alone had
it touch our lips. Our mouths watered. We were hungry to
celebrate this freedom.

Freeing the enslaved—that was the linchpin, right? That
took the wind out of the Confederate sails. I remembered what
Mrs. Beasley had told me: that the South cried out for states'
rights, but this war was really about one thing—whether one
man had the right to own another.

This proclamation had yet to answer that key question
with a resounding *NO*. We were free because our enslavers
lived in a Confederate state. But there were folks in states

bordering the Confederacy who had not left the Union and not renounced slavery—Kentucky, Maryland, Delaware, and Missouri. The status of those people remained unchanged.

And I couldn't help but wonder if this freedom was *real*—could it live and breathe off the page? The Confederacy wouldn't even recognize this proclamation. The eleven states of the Confederacy had their own government, comprised of the Confederate Congress, with Jefferson Davis as president and Alexander Stephens as vice president. Our emancipation meant nothing to them.

The fire crackled, the light growing bright in Edward's eyes. Davis sat on the edge of his chair, his elbows resting on his knees. While the majority of the men sang or shouted "Hurrah," they both looked on in quiet contemplation, sitting on the sidelines of the Proclamation Barbecue.

"You know that fair we passed by a few weeks ago? The one with the magician?" He turned to me, his voice low. "It's all an illusion—this proclamation of emancipation."

"No, don't say that." It was a halfhearted rebuttal. I couldn't hide the fact that I'd been thinking the same thing.

"Hear me out. They make us members of the army but give us these red uniforms. They say they're going to pay us, then offer us half. This promise of freedom is empty."

"Well, I for one wouldn't want to be on the farm right now."

"But is this really better than living with your grand-mother in Savannah? I'm sorry to bring her up."

Just four months ago, Lincoln wanted to ship us back to Africa. To pack us into ships, just as white men forced our ancestors to do, and ship us across the Atlantic. And now that he needed reinforcements for his army, he'd freed us. This seemed like a convenient thing to do to replenish the troops. What would happen after the war? Would the federal government enforce this proclamation? Would they protect us as much as we were protecting them right now?

Because the slaveholders weren't going anywhere. So when that white flag was finally raised, who was going to make sure they complied with this executive order? Who was going to ensure they didn't remain in open rebellion?

"You know what I think? I think we'll win this war. We have the men, the supply lines, the wise old generals. We will win this war, and sooner than we think." Edward turned back to the bonfire, looking queasy. "And then afterward, when the dust settles, we'll be left holding the bag."

I shivered over my stove, stoking the fire for warmth and to make the kettle boil faster. I stared at it, my eyes growing distant in the soft flames. Edward put his hand on my shoulder.

"You know, a watched pot doesn't boil."

"This one better. I'm freezing." And I hadn't had my tea yet. I crouched down and swiped my tin of sassafras root from under my cot. I grabbed my pocketknife and started shaving off bits of root, my hands trembling slightly from the cold. The shavings came off looking like pieces of chipped bark. I looked up at Edward. "Would you like some?"

"No thanks. I don't know how you drink that constantly."

"It's good for you. It's a recipe from my great-great-grandmother, and she lived to be one hundred and twenty years old."

"Come on." Davis poked through the folds of our tent. His husky voice was made huskier by his scratchy throat. He coughed into his shoulder.

"All right, I'm coming." Edward squeezed my shoulder. The sassafras tea wafted into his nostrils, making him scrunch up his nose. "I'll have some when I get back. Maybe."

"Something tells me you won't." I hugged Edward good-bye, lingering a little longer than usual so that I could steal his warmth. Davis slapped Edward on the back. He scratched his chin, which had a smattering of bumps across it. He winced as he scratched it again. "Davis, that's a nasty rash you have."

"It's nothing, just a present from the fleas."

"Yes, they have gotten worse."

"You'd think we'd leave them behind when we move camps, but they only seem to multiply. They seem to love Susie."

"Haha . . . but seriously. Are you sure those are flea bites? I've gotten flea bites before, and those don't look the same. Maybe we should get the doctor to check it out. If you come with me to the field hospital, we could—"

"Perhaps when we get back?" He eyed me the same way Edward had eyed my tea. There was no chance I was getting him anywhere near the hospital—not unless he was flat on his back.

"All right." I shrugged in capitulation. Maybe I was mistaken and he did just have flea bites after all. It wouldn't be the first time I'd made a misdiagnosis. There was still so much I had to learn from the doctor. I was still a novice nurse.

"Come on, we've gotta go." Davis clapped his hands and bounced on the balls of his feet. "Ever since the Confederates got word of the Emancipation Proclamation, they've stepped up their raids."

"Let's push them back!" Edward shouted as he ran off with Davis.

I walked out of our tent, my hands on my hips as I watched them march out. The cold chilled me to the bone, and I wrapped my arms around me. Mary Shaw waved to her husband a few tents away, then turned and looked at me over her shoulder.

"Want to help me with the pies?"

"Yes, I just got more flour from the commissary wagon." I ducked under my tent flap and grabbed the sack of flour I'd received last week. Then I linked arms with Mary as we made our way to the cook tent. There were long tables there we could use for kneading and rolling dough.

The work was nonstop and the pay scant, but working alongside Mary made everything go faster. She had a dry wit that seemed to slice through even dreary situations and make me laugh. But she seemed out of sorts this morning. She fidgeted in our embrace, jostling my shoulders.

"Are you all right?"

"It's nothing," she said as she looked over her shoulder. I followed her gaze and found the boys of Company E marching out of camp.

"They'll be fine, like they always are."

"My husband said they've been meeting a lot of harsh resistance. I just worry about them. Anything can happen in a war." She craned her neck over her shoulder, just to catch one last glimpse of Company E. Then she stilled with a gasp. "Oh my goodness! It's Edward! He's collapsed."

"*My* Edward?" I clutched my chest, scared to the core.

I didn't wait for her to respond. I turned on my heels and dropped the bag of flour near Mary's feet. Then I ran toward the men, who were huddled around someone lying on the ground.

"Edward?" I asked as I pushed past them. When I reached the center of the circle, I found my husband kneeling on the grass over Edward Davis, who was curled into a ball. Davis brought a fist to his mouth, his shoulder hunching through dry heaves as he tried to contain his sickness. But he finally lost the battle, retching out this morning's breakfast onto the ground. My husband scrambled backward, his panicked eyes searching his friend, pleading with me.

"What's wrong with him?" he asked.

"I don't know." I shook my head, searching through my limited medical knowledge. I felt Davis's forehead, and it was hot to the touch. He mumbled something about *not making a fuss*, then groaned as he tried to lift himself off the ground.

"We should help him up and get him to the doctor," one of the boys suggested.

"Wait," I said in a low voice.

It was finally dawning on me what was causing the sickness. Davis had not made it two hundred yards before he collapsed to the ground. A fever and a rash on his face, and he was vomiting. I may not have possessed a sophisticated medical knowledge about most diseases, but I knew these symptoms.

"Step aside, please. Let me examine him." The doctor pushed his way through the crowd, his eyes growing wide with shock. He turned to the uniformed men. "Who has had contact with this man? Just you three? Go to the medical tent immediately. We need to isolate you from the others."

"Is it smallpox, Doctor?" I asked, dreading his confirmation.

"It appears so." The doctor's mouth twisted into a frown as he studied Davis. In the sunlight, his rash looked worse than it had in the shadows of our tent, indicating that his illness was quite advanced.

Edward Davis did not have long to live.

Chapter 14

WE SITUATED DAVIS IN A TENT APART from the rest of the men. The doctor's quarantine protocol had strict rules—only the doctor and the camp steward, James Cummings, were allowed to see or attend to Davis. But I went to see him every day and did my best to nurse him. I wasn't scared of smallpox because I had been vaccinated, and my tea kept me healthy. Davis's isolation was intended to limit the camp's exposure to smallpox, but it did little to quell the anxiety among the men. Several other soldiers fell ill, and people were scared they'd be next.

It was the first time my husband took me up on my offer of sassafras tea. He wanted to try anything to ward off the disease.

The last thing at night, I always went in to see that Davis was comfortable, but in spite of the good care and attention he received, he succumbed to the disease.

I'd seen death before. Death was hard to avoid working as a war nurse. But I'd never seen a friend die. I was with Edward Davis every night for more than a week, saw the glimmer of life in his eyes. And then that light went away. It haunted me to think about his vacant stare, even after we buried him at Camp Saxton.

And when we moved on to Seabrooke, a smaller camp that was eleven miles outside of Beaufort, I was still haunted.

I was deep in thought in the armory, channeling all of my attention to cleaning the regiment's rifles. I carefully disassembled a gun, taking out the cartridges to inspect. They needed to be dry and clean—they needed to shoot straight and true. Any gun in this armory could be the one Edward would shoot. I didn't want to see a misfire or have any blowback. I didn't want Edward to get hurt.

I didn't want to see the light leave his eyes like Edward Davis. We were too young to be dying like this. I set the cartridge down and gripped the tabletop, my knuckles growing white under the strain. A small whimper escaped my lips, catching Mary's attention.

"You all right?" Mary Shaw asked me, looking up from her table of guns.

"Honestly?" I slumped onto the edge of the table. "No. I'm not all right."

"I know." She sighed and put her cartridge down. Then she rounded the front of her table to meet me at mine. "We're all pretty shaken about Davis."

"He was getting better. I was nursing him every night."

"I know. We could smell the sassafras tea all the way over in our tent."

"I did everything right. I wish . . . I wish I could help the others."

Davis had not been the only soldier to fall ill with small-pox. Since the Proclamation Barbecue, the varioloid disease had swept through the camp with a vengeance. It had caused several casualties among our ranks.

And the cold wasn't helping matters. A bitter cold had swept through the Sea Islands. And there was not much cover from the cold in Seabrooke. Unlike Beaufort, where there was a town and fort and infrastructure in place, we only had tents, tall trees, and campfires to keep us warm. And at night, when we needed warmth the most, we had to snuff out our fires. The camp needed to be dark, hidden to the enemy scouts. No light to help them see our location.

"I want to go home."

"But where is home, really?"

I didn't know how to answer Mary. The last place that truly felt like home was my grandmother's tiny house in Savannah. Our half-life between being enslaved and being free hadn't been an easy one, but it was still *home*. It had only been a year since I'd left Savannah, but it felt like a lifetime.

"Beaufort was the last home we really had." I shrugged, considering the distance to our last camp. It wasn't so far away. "I left some dried herbs and flour there. My blankets and a few books, thinking we'd be back there before long."

"But the war hasn't panned out that way. The boys need to remain here to help the general. Oh! But there is a commissary wagon that goes to Beaufort. We could hitch a ride with it. Would you like that?"

The plan unfolded in my mind. We could walk the familiar streets of Beaufort, see old friends who had stayed behind. And I could retrieve some of my belongings I'd left with my former neighbor. Such a trip might lift my spirits. A small smile tugged at my lips.

"I'll take that as a yes?"

"Yes. I'd like that very much indeed."

It was still early, and the commissary wagon was likely still there. We could rush to catch it and be back at our former camp by about one o'clock. Then it was only a two-mile walk to my old quarters. We could be in and out of there within a couple hours and be back in time to meet the wagon again by three o'clock that afternoon.

I picked up my skirts and turned toward the tent opening with a wide grin.

"Let's go!"

As predicted, we reached Beaufort just after noon that day. And after a brisk two-mile walk to our former camp, I felt warmer and lighter, like the distance from Seabrooke had restored my good nature. Our bags were full with our belongings and tasty treats our friends had gifted us.

"This is good," I said, dipping my finger in a jar of blackberry jam. "*Really* good. Phyllis has outdone herself this time."

"I'm shocked." Mary chuckled as we walked down the road back to the center of town. "Remember when she first came to camp? She couldn't cook a thing."

"She would have burned water if I'd left her alone for too long."

Mary laughed. "You speak the truth."

"Thank you for this. I needed to get away."

"Me too."

We reached the town square, right where the commissary wagon had dropped us off. After it made the rounds to the other soldiers and shops, it would depart from this very spot. The sun was lower on the horizon, indicating early afternoon.

"Where is that wagon?"

"Excuse me, sir?" I approached an elderly gentleman selling pecans by the roadside. "Do you have the time?"

"Yes, ma'am." He nodded at me, then pulled his pocket watch out of his apron. "It's just about half past three."

"Oh." My smile faded. "Oh—thank you."

"We've missed it, haven't we?" Mary stomped her foot then grunted in frustration. "I knew we stayed too long visiting with Phyllis."

"What are we going to do?" The commissary wagon didn't run between camp every day. It could be days until the next wagon arrived. Sure, we could stay with our friends at our old camp, but I didn't want to worry Edward. He'd just lost a friend. I didn't want to disappear on him too. I slapped my arms at my sides, jostling my bag of belongings. "We'll have to walk back."

"Walk?" Mary's mouth hung open. Then she cupped her hands over her eyes and snuck a peek at where the sun hung near the horizon. I knew what she was going to say—that we couldn't walk this late in the day. That it was unsafe without a proper escort. She reached out for my hand. "Susie, let's just—"

Before she had a chance to suggest we remain in Beaufort, I sidestepped her outstretched hand and headed down the road leading out of town. The gravel crunched behind me as Mary tried to keep up.

"Ain't no sense in standing around talking about it. We can do this. It's three thirty. The sun will set in a couple of hours. That's enough time to get back."

"For someone who knows their numbers, you're not doing the math right." She jogged ahead of me and turned on her heels, walking backward so that she could face me while she spoke. "It's at least ten miles to Seabrooke!"

"I have to get back to Edward, okay?" I said desperately, my whole expression pleading with her.

Her eyes burned indignantly at me. I could tell she was warring with competing emotions—should she stay behind for a few days or join me on my journey? If she did the former option, she'd leave me to walk back to Seabrooke on my own.

And that was something my protective friend would never do. She turned back again without another word to me.

Her arms pumped at her sides as she stomped down the road. Anger and frustration practically rippled off of her hunched shoulders.

The sun was getting low, and we grew more frightened, fearful of meeting some animal or of treading on a snake in our way. We did not meet a person, and we were frightened almost to death. Our feet were so sore, we could hardly walk.

The sun sank lower in the sky. It seemed to sink faster as it approached the horizon. The shadows of early evening crept down the walkway until finally a true darkness had set upon us.

"How far do you think we've walked?" Mary asked me as she slowed down. It was the first thing she'd said in hours. I was grateful to hear something other than our breathy huffing.

"Must be about eight miles, surely." I leaned against a neighboring tree trunk, moaning as I took some of the weight off my feet.

"These are not the right shoes to be doing all this walking." Mary tugged at her laces and kicked off her shoes. Her stockinged feet rested on the gravel.

"If only they'd issued us boots like they did for the men." I pulled my shoes off too and rubbed at my sore feet. I looked around.

There we were, nothing around us but dense woods. The

darkness in those woods was blacker than black, more sinister and scary-looking than I'd ever seen before.

I stowed my shoes in my bag and started walking again, feeling the grit and grime of the gravel road digging into my stockings. I didn't dare look back at Mary. I could hear her walking behind me without her shoes, hear the soft crunch of gravel. I knew if I looked back at her, I'd see her scowl.

And maybe I deserved her censure.

It was quite dangerous to be out here in the dark. Two women alone at night—any horror could befall them. There could be wolves or, worse yet, rebels in these deep woods. The South did not recognize the Emancipation Proclamation, so we were just fugitives who could be recaptured and re-enslaved.

We shouldn't have been out here.

The road curved in a familiar way, and my heart rate quickened. I recognized this bend—we were close to Seabrooke.

"There!" I pointed in front of me. The picket line of our troops was just ahead.

"Help!" Mary shouted, hobbling forward to meet them.

Walking in our stockings had made the pain in our feet worse.

"Stop right there!" a voice yelled through the darkness. "We are authorized to shoot on sight."

And I knew they meant business. Sometimes, late at night, an errant shot would slice through the air, likely one of our boys shooting a possible infiltrator. The Confederate troops tested our fortifications. And they knew that our commanding officer accepted deserters in his camp.

Sometimes Confederate soldiers would raise a white flag of truce, posing as deserters, just so they could come nearer to the Union camp and scope out our headquarters. It was a ruse, of course. They'd soon disappear from our camp and tell the rebel troops what they'd learned.

That is what these soldiers thought we were—a Confederate ruse. After not seeing us by dusk, they'd concluded we had decided to remain over until next day and therefore had no idea of our plight. Imagine their surprise when we reached camp about eleven p.m.

The guard challenged us. "Who comes there?"

My answer was, "A friend without a countersign."

He approached and saw who it was, reported, and we were admitted into the lines.

Then he howled in laughter. "What in the Sam Hill happened to you?"

Chapter 15

THE BOYS WERE STILL HOWLING WITH LAUGHter by the week's end, when we packed up camp to march on Jacksonville, Florida. We left Camp Saxton in March of 1863 between four and five o'clock and arrived at Jacksonville about eight o'clock the next morning, accompanied by three or four gunboats. When the rebels saw these boats, they ran out of the city, leaving the women behind, and we found out afterward that they'd thought we had a much larger fleet than we really had.

The thrill of advancing to yet another state was dulled by the fact that I was still the butt end of a joke.

"There's our little deserter!"

Mary gripped her bag, holding it tightly to her chest, and stalked off to the edge of the bulk of the march. She was still quite sore with me about our trek from Beaufort to Seabrooke. And Edward was too.

When I'd gotten home that night, he said he was just happy to see me and to know that I was safe. But his nostrils flared like he was frustrated with my foolishness.

"We thought y'all were rebel soldiers disguised as women. Who else would be out in the middle of the night?"

"Sergeant King, have you checked to see that's not soot on her face?" another soldier joked.

"All right, all right." Edward chuckled along with them. Then he gave me a sidelong glance. His nostrils flared, and then he turned his attention back to the road.

"Hold on." Captain Trowbridge held up his fist, signaling for our company to stop. He lengthened his spyglass and pointed it toward the center of Jacksonville, Florida.

On the horizon, smoke billowed in large chunks of the sky. All of it stemmed from the city of Jacksonville, where our gunboats along the coast had their cannons fixed. Another cannon fired, sending a sonic boom whirring through the air.

We often traveled with the company of at least one gunboat. They primed the cities we marched on—warning them that Union foot soldiers were not far away. The Confederate Army had two choices—stay and fight, or turn tail and get out alive while they still could. Evidently, the enemy had chosen to abandon their post this time.

What was left of the Confederate Army was likely

destroying properties of value. Better to leave a pile of charred ash than to allow the Union Army any useful infrastructure.

"We have the enemy on the run." The officer smiled smugly. "Looks like the city is ours."

A collective cheer thundered through the ranks.

"Company E, you know the drill. We take the left flank and try to get any of the surrounding stragglers. Approach any flag of truce with caution, but you may choose to honor it if you believe it to be genuine. Fall out."

I gave Edward's hand one last squeeze and then released it. I filed out of the ranks along with some of the other nurses and wives, then watched as the boys filed out in the direction of the outskirts of town. I swallowed a lump in my throat. Sometimes I thought the small skirmishes that happened in the bushes were more dangerous than battle in an open field. The enemy knew this area better than the Union troops. They got scrappier and stealthier, spurred on by the desperation of a lost battle.

I shuffled down the road, moving slowly. Our tiny caravan of nurses, cooks, and support staff was in no hurry to get to town. And I for one was relieved to have a break from all the jokes about my harrowing walk from Beaufort to Seabrooke. I worried that I'd never live that down.

Lizzie nudged my side with her elbow.

"The boys are just having their fun," she said as if she could hear my thoughts.

"Every time they bring it up, I swear Edward's head is going to explode," I grumbled under my breath.

"He'll forgive you in time." Lizzie smiled encouragingly. Then her eyes flitted ahead of the caravan to where Mary Shaw was walking. "And she'll forgive and forget too. In good time."

I hoped she would. This life on the road was a lonely one. We'd all left family behind to be here. We were each other's family. I needed Mary in my life.

The men ran off to the left of the city instead of continuing down the main road. That would be too easy—the Confederate soldiers would be watching this road, and they'd be ready to attack. But our soldiers would ambush the enemy from the sides of the city, causing the Confederates to fight on all fronts. Hopefully the battle would be over by the end of the day.

Our group of women and support staff kept to the main road, moving leisurely so that the soldiers had time to clear out the outlying houses of rebel soldiers. A small home sat at the base of the hill, not far from the heart of Jacksonville. A pair of women and three children stood outside on the porch, looking at the smoky sky above their city.

"Good afternoon." Lizzie nodded and smiled in greeting.

"Good afternoon," I echoed.

One woman gave a curt nod in response. The other spit on the ground between us.

"We were wondering if you might have some food you

could spare." Lizzie wrapped her shawl tighter around her shoulders, smiling stiffly. "We've been traveling for days and have had to make do with limited rations."

"We don't have anything but some hardtack," the other woman said as she clutched the children at her sides. She was frightened of us. But we were a group of unarmed women— there was nothing to fear except the color of our skin. And I supposed that was enough for her.

"May we please have some, ma'am?" I asked as politely as I could muster. It was clear that they didn't want us anywhere near their home, but surely they could spare a few crackers.

"Look around you. Haven't y'all taken enough?" The woman who'd spat pointed to the haze of smoke billowing in the distance. "We can't spare none of it for you."

"Don't have nothin' for you people." The other woman flicked her hand at us, shooing us away. "Now, go on, git. *Git!*"

Her grimace sliced right through me. She was so bitterly against our people and had no mercy or sympathy for us.

"Come on," I said, tugging on Lizzie's sleeve. It was clear we weren't going to get any sustenance from the residents of this house—or from the residents of Jacksonville. Their hatred for us endured even with their city's surrender.

I wondered if the people of the Confederacy would ever accept our kind on their doorsteps.

Once the city of Jacksonville was secured, our regiment doubled back and headed up to South Carolina. To me, it seemed like we were going around in circles. But I trusted the generals and captains to lead us in the right direction. They hadn't led us astray yet.

And there was something in my bones that told me our side was winning.

I could see the weariness and anger on the Confederate soldiers' faces as they looked at us from across the river. We were camped just outside of Barnwell Plantation, not far from Hall Island. On one side of the river was our camp, teaming with Black soldiers—all of us free people. On the other side was the Confederate Army, who looked on at us with unabashed hatred.

I walked down the picket line, as I did most evenings. I had a fresh basket of bread from the cook tent, and at the bottom of my basket were small pies for sale. I walked in the direction of the officers' tent, as they had the discretionary income to purchase cakes and pies. The bread was free for anyone who asked. I carefully wove through the ranks, providing the boys in blue with sustenance. I was handing over a bread roll to a soldier when a shot sliced through the air.

"Goodness!" I flinched. I whipped my head to watch the gray and grim soldiers on the other side. Another shot rang through the air, piercing the middle of the river. I mumbled under my breath, "You're going to have to cross the river to get to this side. And you don't want to do that!"

"Please. A bit of bread," yelled one of the Confederate soldiers. "Throw it over."

I shook my head. If a fast-traveling bullet couldn't make it over the wide mouth of the river, there was no way I could get a basket of bread to travel any farther.

"Don't mind them." Edward gave my shoulder a reassuring squeeze while he looked across the river. "They've been doing that all morning."

"They must be desperate to be asking me to send food over."

"Begging us for food isn't so unthinkable when your belly is empty."

"With all this farmland down here, you'd think they could at least feed their troops."

"Not with us disrupting their supply lines, they can't." Edward smiled slyly. "We've had more deserters than we've ever gotten before. Some of them are plain hungry and tired of the rigors of war. Others claim they have no slaves to fight for."

I crossed my arms and turned away from the starving soldiers on the other side. A gulf separated us from one another—and I wasn't just talking about the river that separated our two camps. We were on completely different sides of Emancipation. But that didn't mean their suffering didn't affect me.

This war was chopping all of us down, regardless of who was winning and who was losing. I just wanted it to be over.

* * *

The cold was so piercing, it cut right to my bones. It was the winter of 1864, and I was already wearing everything I owned—two pairs of socks, three bloomers underneath my thickest wool skirt, and a thick shawl over my shoulders. I unfurled the blanket I'd haphazardly folded at the foot of my cot and wrapped it around my shoulders. We were stationed at Camp Shaw, but we were continuously on the move, making it difficult to remember where we were on any given month.

I knelt before my small fire, getting so close to the flames that I could feel the heat singe my eyebrows. But I didn't care. I needed to find warmth before I slipped into hypothermia. The doctor taught me that hypothermia happened when your body temperature dipped so low that your organs stopped functioning. It sounded like a gruesome way to go.

I wouldn't let that happen to me.

A bugle played, reminding us all to extinguish our lights throughout the camp. That melancholic, stoic rhythm was our call to bed. Then the provost guard blew his whistle, which sounded right outside my canvas door, and I knew what time it was—lights out. We had to follow the rules and extinguish our lights.

I looked longingly at my fire. I didn't want it to go out and take all the warmth with it. And then an idea struck me.

I scrambled to my knees and slid my mess pan from underneath my bed. A mess pan is made of sheet iron, something like a roasting pan, only they are nearly as large around as a peck measure, but not so deep.

Then I scratched the cold, hard ground with my fingers until I finally broke the surface. I scooped up the dirt and put it into the bottom of the pan. In the morning, I could go to the cook shed, fill it nearly full of coals, and carry it back to my tent. But for now, I'd have to make do with my own embers.

Carefully I scooped up my embers and placed them on my dirt-lined mess pan. As a lid, I used one of my other pans. The makeshift metal furnace radiated heat throughout the tent. It was moments like these that I realized how the war had turned me into many things: a teacher, a nurse, and an engineer.

The same bugle that had just put the camp to bed was now playing a rallying cry to wake us. As the sun chased away the chill, my concerns about cold nights seemed foolish. For the past three years, men had lost their lives every day fighting this war. I tried to remind myself of this every time I complained about my cold tent. Rations were low, and everything was difficult to come by. We did our best to make do with what we had, and when blessings came in different forms, we appreciated them.

While at Camp Shaw, I visited the hospital in Beaufort and pitched in however I could. The noise and the bustle were overwhelming—the hospital was teeming with activity. Because there weren't enough rooms to house the constant influx of patients, cots lined the hallway to handle the overflow. Those cots were filled now. In some places, there were double rows of cots.

Even above the noise of the hospital, the firing could be plainly heard in the distance. I hastened down to the hallway, trying to find a way to be of use. I recognized faces along the way. Samuel Anderson of our company was badly wounded, but he was being tended to by a doctor. He was in better hands than most of the men, who were struggling to stay conscious with all kinds of unimaginable wounds.

I rounded the corner to the stairway and hustled down the steps. When I reached the landing, I saw an even more gruesome display of the atrocities of war. The injuries were worse than the blown-off limbs from upstairs. The lobby was set up as a surgery, cleared of cots and extraneous personnel. A woman leaned over an operating table, joined by one of the doctors, who was administering a syringe to the patient's veins.

"Who is she?" I asked another nurse. "I haven't seen her before."

"That's Clara Barton." A flicker of a smile flashed across her face. "They call her the Angel of the Battlefield. She came just the other day with a whole bunch of supplies to replenish our stores."

Medical supplies were in short supply most of the time. But now, thanks to Clara, we had restocked.

The doctor's arm shot out to the nurse beside him. He wiggled his fingers expectantly.

"Here, I can help." I stepped in, eager to be of assistance.

Chapter 16

THE SHEETS RUSTLED IN THE COT NEXT TO me. I peered out of the corner of my eyes to where Mary slept. But she was clearly not sleeping. Instead, she was scratching her scalp with a vigor she usually reserved for laundry.

"I can't take this anymore!" She threw her blankets on the floor. Swinging her legs over the side of her bed, she sat up, then scratched her forearm. "How do you not have fleas?"

"Oh, I have fleas." I reached farther into my blanket and scratched my ankle. "They've been biting me all night."

"I haven't slept a wink!"

"I know. I don't know why I'm even trying to sleep anymore." I swung my legs over the edge of my bed and hopped up. "I'm going to go walk to the fort. You may join me if you want."

"No thank you—not after what happened the last time we went for a walk. We ended up lost in the woods and getting back to camp in the middle of the night."

"We weren't lost."

"Whatever you say." She tutted around the tent, busying herself with folding discarded clothing instead of making eye contact with me.

"You're never going to let me live that one down." When she shook her head, I sighed in capitulation. I smiled playfully and shrugged. "Suit yourself then."

I scratched the back of my neck as I walked to the edge of camp, which hugged the coastline of Morris Island. This island was a narrow strip of sandy soil, nothing growing on it but a few bushes and shrubs. The camp was one mile from the boat landing, called Pawnell Landing, close to Fort Wagner.

The fleas had been bad at camp ever since we'd moved here. I took comfort in the fact that Edward wasn't here to experience the worst fleas of the war. And the vain part of me was relieved that he didn't have to see the scratch marks all over my body.

But I missed him. I worried about him.

At the top of the bluffs I could just make out the ramparts of Fort Wagner, which stood a few miles down the beach. The fort was now in Union control, a strategic win for our cause. Coupled with the support of the gunboats in the Atlantic Ocean, they were a formidable force for the Confederate troops to fend off.

The fort and the gunboats had turned the might of their guns against Charleston. The ground shook beneath my feet as they fired toward the city. They shelled every fifteen minutes. It had become almost routine to me, but my heart still leapt through my chest almost every time I felt the impact reverberate through the bay.

Somewhere on the other end of those cannonballs was a person.

Something hard cracked beneath my boots. When I looked down, I saw a hard, matte-white shard that was smooth to the touch. It was bone.

Human bone.

Along the ramparts, bits of bone and human skulls littered the walkway outside of the fort. I knelt down and picked up one of the skulls. My fingers trembled as I looked at the cracked skull. I set it just off the pathway in the patchy grass and sand. It wasn't a proper burial, but at least it was out of the flow of traffic.

Then my eyes surveyed the path ahead—more human skulls. They were a gruesome sight, those fleshless heads and grinning jaws, but by this time I had become accustomed to worse things and did not feel as I might have earlier in my camp life. It seems strange how our aversion to seeing suffering is overcome in war, how we are able to see the most sickening sights, such as men with their limbs blown off and mangled by the deadly shells, without a shudder, and instead of turning away, how we hurry to assist in alleviating their pain, bind up their wounds, and press the cool water to their parched lips, with feelings only of sympathy and pity.

My throat seized and I almost broke out in tears. So many lives were lost on this very spot. It was an eerie, sobering display of the destruction of war.

"Who are you?" I asked one of the other skulls I picked up. It stared silently back at me as I nestled it in the tall grass. "Which side did you fight for?"

Maybe they were Confederates who'd fought and failed to hold Fort Wagner from the advancing Union troops. Or maybe these skulls belonged to Union soldiers who'd fought trying to take the fort.

Or maybe these fallen soldiers belonged to both sides of this war, death being the great equalizer.

Part of me wished I could tell who was a Confederate and who was a Union soldier, so that I could know who to pray for. But another part of me—a very small part—knew that wasn't the right way to look at the skulls of Morris Island.

The war brought death. Slavery brought death. And the sooner this war ended, the sooner slavery ended, the sooner this country would have a chance at rebirth.

For the rest of the day, I avoided my tent at all costs—the fleas were that bad. Instead, I spent the afternoon cooking outside. I'd long since run out of flour to make cakes and pies. I'd used the last of it in Beaufort, and since then, we'd been on the move, changing locations to more isolated locales, and there wasn't a store around us to barter in or trade for ingredients.

All I had left were a few cans of condensed milk, a cube of sugar, and some turtle eggs I'd foraged the other day. It wasn't much to look at—definitely not what the men asked for while they lay in their sickbeds. They wanted soup or salted beef, something warm and filling. But I had an idea for something else.

Outside of my tent, the pot of turtle eggs and canned milk simmered on the edge of my rock-lined firepit. I didn't want to place my concoction in the center of the fire, because then it would burn too hot and overcook the eggs. So I set it on the edge of the flames and turned the pot every few minutes so that it was evenly heated on all sides.

"Post." Mary rambled up the aisle of tents, waving an envelope in her hand.

"For me?" I asked, raising my eyebrow. It was November of 1864, and it had been a while since I'd received mail from Edward. I just chalked it up to supply-line interruptions. But as Mary drew closer to me, I could see the smile tugging at her lips. I had mail!

I sprang up from my perch on the ground and ran toward her. I snatched the letter from her hand, my hasty fingers ripping at the envelope's seam before I'd had a chance to catch my breath.

"Well, what's it say?" Mary said, breathing heavily. She must have run all the way from the commissary tent, which was on the other side of camp, not far from the ramparts of Fort Wagner. She stepped behind me, trying to read the letter over my shoulder.

"Sergeant King says the boys were still lying three miles from Gregg Landing, and they still haven't had a fight yet; that the rebels were waiting on them and they on the rebels, and each were holding their own," I read. "Also, that General Sherman has taken Fort McAllister, eight miles from Savannah."

"Well, that's good that they haven't seen much fighting."

"Where is Gregg Landing?" I wracked my brain. We'd been to so many different forts and campsites, it was often hard to keep them straight. But I was pretty sure I knew where it was. I tilted my head to the side.

Mary rested her hand on my shoulder. "Edward is fine. I can feel these things."

"It's been far too long since I've seen him. I've gotta get to Beaufort."

"Wait a minute. This sounds like another one of your crazy plans. Getting to Beaufort from out here on Morris Island will take days."

"So what you're saying is it's not impossible."

"I'm saying . . . I think you should stay here. I'm not going with you this time. When we walked back from Beaufort to Seabrooke, it nearly killed us."

"I know, and I've learned a lot from that experience. Look, I'm not asking you to come with me this time. I would love it if you did but understand if you won't. But I *have* to be near Edward. I need to be able to nurse him back to health if he gets injured."

"All right, then." Mary nodded. "Let's get you a travel pass and get you on that commissary wagon to Hilton Head. It's the only way you'll get to Beaufort."

Chapter 17

WHEN I ARRIVED AT HILTON HEAD AT about three o'clock next day, there was a flurry of activity following a recent battle with the Confederate Army. A steamer floated at the dock, and a crowd of nurses and orderlies was unloading stretchers of wounded men. I fought my instinct to roll my sleeves up and help with the wounded soldiers. I had to get to Edward. He needed me too.

I wove my way through the hubbub, searching for the charter that ran from Hilton Head to Beaufort. Someone tugged on my sleeve, stopping me in my tracks. I wrenched my arm away, prepared to grumble at whoever had waylaid me, but I recognized the man immediately.

"Hello, Doctor!" I was grateful to meet a familiar face in all the commotion.

"I thought that was you, Mrs. King." He wiped his brow with the back of his hand. "We could use your help at the hospital. As you can see, it's all hands on deck today."

"I—" I stammered, finding it difficult to turn him down. I breathed deeply, then shook my head. "I'm sorry, I can't stay. I am on the way to Beaufort to be with my husband."

"But you can't get to Beaufort." His eyebrows crinkled as he gestured to the steamer behind him. "The naval yacht cannot dock until we get these men offloaded. Truly we could use your help, at least until Monday."

"I'll inquire about a transfer myself," I said, backing away. "Really, I must be going. I am so sorry."

I tightened my knapsack around my shoulder and marched down the dock before the doctor had a chance to protest. I was anxious to get off, as I knew no one at Hilton Head.

At the other end of the dock stood a queue of a few passengers facing the water, somewhat removed from the commotion of the steamer. I walked over to a woman holding a young child who could not be more than two years old.

"Excuse me, is this the line for transfer to Beaufort?"

"Yes, it is." She repositioned the child in her arms so that she could see me better. She had bags under her eyes and sunken cheeks. She looked exhausted. "I'm Mrs. Walker, Corporal Walker's wife. And you are?"

"I'm Susie King, Sergeant King's wife. He's not far from Beaufort. Do you think we'll be able to get there before the end of the day?"

"No idea." She sighed and then gave a small shrug. "They're trying to see if they can get the yacht to shore, but it might be a while because they need to tend to the wounded. There are also five smaller boats that can carry people over. Maybe we'll get lucky with one of those."

I circulated among the group, trying to gather more information. The only people here besides Corporal Walker's wife were Mrs. Lizzie Brown, who had come over on a permit to see her gravely ill husband; a woman named Mrs. Seabrooke; a comrade just discharged; and an officer's boy.

We waited for hours at the end of the dock. Our journey could not take precedence over the wounded soldiers and the other naval transport vessels that were ferrying fresh ammunition and manpower. It was nearly dark by the time the yacht moored at the Hilton Head dock. The sky was an ominous dark gray.

A storm was brewing, and it wouldn't make our voyage easy.

The ramp up to the yacht was wobbly under the force of the current. I had to grip the railing with both of my hands just to make it across safely. I looked behind me at Mrs. Walker, who was struggling to traverse the treacherous walkway. I stepped back onto the ramp, prepared to run and assist her, but the discharged officer scurried across to help her and her child.

Once we were all aboard, the yacht charted a course through the choppy waters between Hilton Head and Beaufort.

As we got farther into open water, the swells seemed to get bigger. Every wave thrashed and tossed the yacht around like it was a mere child's toy and not a formidable vessel.

At about eight o'clock, a wave of water came barreling toward us. And this time the yacht tipped over so far on its side that it could not bounce back. I slid across the deck, my desperate fingers struggling to find something to hold on to. I gripped the railing just as the boat was trying to right itself.

But it had taken on too much water. The boat groaned against the pressure from the excess weight. And that's when we truly started to go down.

I knew in that moment that there was no recovering from this.

I caught hold of the sail and managed to hold fast. Mrs. Walker held on to her child with one hand, while with the other she managed to grasp some other part of the boat, and we drifted and shouted as loud as we could, trying to attract the attention of some of the government boats, which were going up and down the channel.

"Help!" I screamed at a ship in the distance. Water sloshed in my mouth, but I kept screaming. "HELP."

But it was in vain; we could not make ourselves heard. I hugged the sail mast, holding on for dear life, feeling my hope slip away. The waves jostled me from side to side, rattling my resolve.

This was how I was going to die.

Just when we gave up all hope, and in the last moment

(as we thought) gave one more despairing cry, someone shouted back.

"Over here!" I splashed around toward the voice, slapping the water with one hand while holding on to the sail with my other. I had learned the basics of swimming while on St. Simons Island, but I still was not a great swimmer. And I was fully clothed in the water. If I let go of the mast, my water-logged boots and dress would take me under. I was sure of it.

Another cry in response came from the direction of Lady's Island. Two boats were put off and a search was made to locate our distressed boat. They found us at last, nearly dead from exposure. In fact, the poor little baby was dead, although her mother still held her by her clothing with her teeth. The soldier was drowned, having been caught under the sail and pinned down.

But the rest of us were saved.

One of the rescuers lifted me out of the water. I collapsed in his arms, unable to walk, thoroughly exhausted. We were given the best attention that we could get at this place where we were picked up.

The men who saved us were surprised when they found me among the passengers, as one of them, William Geary, was a friend of my husband and was from Edward's home-town of Darien, Georgia. His mother lived about two miles from where we were picked up. She had heard cries for a long time that night and was very uneasy about it. He recounted the conversation he'd had with her before he found us.

She'd said to her son, "I think some poor souls are cast away."

"I don't think so, Mother," he'd replied. "I saw some people going down the river today. You know this is Christmas, they're just having a good time."

She persisted that these were cries of distress and not of joy, and begged him to go out and see. So to satisfy her, he went outside and listened, and then he heard them also, and hastened to get the boats off to find us.

I blinked awake to find Edward leaning over me. His smile was tight as he brushed the side of my cheek with his fingers.

"Why do you insist on these dangerous adventures?" he grumbled under his breath, shifting in his seat so that he could lean closer to me. "And just to see me on Christmas Day?"

"Edward," I said, my voice sounding raspy and strained. A sob escaped my lips. "Edward, of course I came to be with you on Christmas. Why wouldn't I?"

"It's all right. I'm here."

"I was so worried about you." I coughed loudly.

"I think I should be worried about you right now. The doctor said you were exposed to the elements for quite a while. That cough sounds awful."

"I'm fine." I brushed away his hands, uncomfortable being a patient. I'd knocked my head pretty badly, but I was still able to get up after a short rest. I rose from the bed, trying to get onto my feet, but Edward put a firm hand on my shoulder.

"Sit. Down." He said each word deliberately, slowly, so that I'd know he meant business. "Let me nurse you for a change. This is my Christmas gift to you."

I sank down to my covers and chuckled under my breath. The image of Edward being a nurse in a white apron brought lightness to my weary spirit.

"How you can laugh at a time like this is beyond me." He rolled his eyes and pulled away from me. "You were struggling in the water for four hours last night. You swallowed so much salt water that the doctor said you nearly drowned."

"Four hours? No, that can't be right. I screamed for help, and William Geary appeared within an hour or so."

"No, Susie. Your boat capsized around eight fifteen p.m., and it was near midnight when they found you."

"How is Corporal Walker's wife?" I asked, my voice low.

"She is distraught, of course. She lost her child." He crossed his arms and cast his stony gaze out of the window. "Had the tide been going out, you would have been carried to sea and lost."

"Oh." I let that sobering fact sit with me for a while.

"I don't know if you had anything more than your knapsack with you. We've been keeping a sharp lookout on the beach for anything that might wash in from the yacht, but we've only managed to retrieve a trunk and some smaller things."

"Edward, I have everything I need right here."

"Please don't ever do anything that reckless again, okay?

You've been saved by the grace of God *twice*. First after your midnight walk to Seabrooke with Mary Shaw. And now this." He sighed wearily. "You're not to leave my side again, understood?"

I nodded. That sounded good to me.

"As soon as you're surefooted, you're going to Cole Island, where you can be attended by Dr. Miner. It'll get you out of the hot zone of war, and I know he'll do everything in his power to alleviate your suffering. You are still quite swollen. But I don't know what he can do with that cough. It sounds so severe."

"It's fine . . . it'll be fine." I coughed again. "See, it's better already."

Chapter 18

BY THE END OF FEBRUARY, I WAS WELL enough to continue my duties with the regiment, although I still had a lingering cough that just wouldn't leave, no matter what Dr. Miner gave me. I tried to hide the cough from Edward, but that was hard, given that we spent most of our time together. He wanted to keep me cooped up until the cough passed, but finally I convinced him that I was well enough to travel, and we rejoined the regiment, which had been ordered to Charleston on February 28, 1865. Our scouts had reported back to our commanding office that there were signs of the rebels evacuating that city.

Charleston, a great stronghold of the Confederacy, was falling.

Leaving Cole Island, we arrived in Charleston between nine and ten o'clock in the morning and found the Confederate troops had set fire to the city and fled, leaving women and children behind to suffer and perish in the flames. The fire engulfed almost the entire city. It burned fiercely for a whole day and night.

It was a lot to take in after being in recovery for so long. I had almost forgotten what a grisly business war was. I sat next to Edward outside of our tent and watched the flames rip the city apart.

It was a terrible scene.

The next day, we marched toward the charred remains of Charleston. Under a flag of truce, our regiment went to work assisting the citizens in subduing the flames. For three or four days the men fought the fire, saving the property and effects of the people.

It was often thankless work. The white men and women could not tolerate the fact we were now free people. Many among our ranks had formerly been their slaves. Although these brave men risked life and limb to assist them in their distress, white men and even women would sneer and harass them whenever they met them.

I was assigned quarters at a residence on South Battery Street, one of the most aristocratic parts of the city. Staying in such a fine house seemed to enrage the locals even more. Black Union soldiers sleeping in rich white peoples' beds did not sit well with them.

But it was the best place to set up the hospital while we worked to save their city from continued outbursts of fires.

There, I assisted in caring for the sick and injured soldiers of our regiment.

After Charleston was firmly controlled by Union troops, we moved through the region, putting out small fires everywhere. The whole South seemed to be in flames. Finally, news came from Appomattox, Virginia.

Big news.

Gripping the day's newspaper in my hand, I ran down the street toward Edward's post on the south end of the city. The pages fluttered in the wind as I picked up my pace, dodging charred debris and discarded belongings in the otherwise empty street. This news was sure to bring Edward absolute joy. As I reached the end of the block, I saw him in the distance, standing dutifully at his post.

"Edward!" I yelled down the street. "Edward!"

He turned in my direction, a look of confusion and concern on his face as he watched me running toward him. His legs twitched as if he was going to run and meet me halfway, but as he could not abandon his post, he stayed planted to the spot, looking more nervous than ever.

"Edward." I skidded to a stop, struggling to catch my breath.

"What is it? What's happened? Are you all right?"

"Here," I said, shoving the newspaper in his hands.

His lips moved as he read the headline. A cautious smile crossed his lips, then he yelled over his shoulder, "Boys, come here! You're gonna want to hear this."

"What's this about?" One of his fellow guards looked at the paper over his shoulder. He squinted at the words on the page then shook his head. "What's it say?"

"It says that Confederate General Robert E. Lee surrendered to General Ulysses S. Grant on April 9, 1865. I will read it: 'Surrender of Lee and his whole army to General Grant. Lee sues for peace! Entire destruction of rebel power in Virginia. The war virtually ended and the Union restored.'"

"So . . . the war is over?" the soldier asked.

"Yes," I replied. "Well, virtually over—whatever that means."

"You hear that, boys? The war is over!" He threw his cap in the air, his feet doing a little jig in the street. His elation was palpable and contagious. Soon the rest of the officers in the vicinity joined in the celebration.

The war was *virtually* over. I wasn't sure why the newspaper had qualified it in that way. It lacked the finality we were craving. But for now, it was enough to lift our spirits.

Victory was ours.

There were some in the South who didn't respect the surrender of their leader. The war was technically over, but we were taking fire daily. These rebellious forces, who did not recognize the end of the war, were called bushwhackers. They hid in the bushes and shot at us every chance they got. Other times they would conceal themselves in the train cars used to transfer our soldiers, and when our boys, worn out and tired, fell asleep, these men would come out from their hiding places and cut their throats. Several of our men were killed in this way. We could not figure out who was committing these murders, until one night one of the rebels was caught in the act trying to cut the throat of a sleeping soldier.

There was no reasoning with this rebel. He would not accept the end of the war.

He was put under guard, court-martialed, and shot at Wall Hollow. First Lieutenant Jerome T. Furman and a number of soldiers were killed by these South Carolina bushwhackers at Wall Hollow. After this man was shot, however, the regiment marched back to Charleston unharmed.

When we got back to the big city, we were confronted with terrible news—President Lincoln had been shot and killed on April 14, just days after Robert E. Lee's surrender. The news deflated the entire regiment, and morale went to an all-time low.

If the president of the United States wasn't safe, I wondered if Black people would ever feel secure in this precarious peace.

The bushwhackers continued fighting, complicating the end of the war. Because of them, there was no clean finish to the fighting. Every time we thought things were settling down, another skirmish would commence.

These fits and starts of war were quite exhausting.

We battled for nearly a full year after Robert E. Lee's surrender, fighting roving bands of bushwhackers. Their strong-holds were outside of major cities, particularly in the country, where their isolation from the influence of outsiders enabled some plantations to continue business as usual.

The system of slavery still endured in many parts of the South *after* Emancipation and the capitulation of the Confederate States of America, which meant that when we marched through the rural counties, there were people who believed they were still in bondage. Their enslavers had not informed them of their freedom. If anything, they had stepped up their enforcement of slavery, desperately grasping on to a system that was over.

We made it our mission to liberate as many people as possible by telling them of the Emancipation Proclamation, about the end of the war, and about a life of liberty and freedom. But after we marched on to the next town, I wondered what would become of these newly freed people.

They had no money to show for their years of service to their former owners, no plot of land to call their own. In theory they were free, but in practice, they were still tied to the land.

In February of 1866, almost a year after the formal end of the war, my regiment received our orders to muster out. Lieutenant Colonel Trowbridge had been promoted several times from when we first met him. Our former captain—now colonel—wrote a touching letter to us on our last day of service to the Union Army.

Mary, Lizzie, and I sat outside of the cook tent on Morris Island, weary from years of free service to the country. Mary had learned to read during her time in Company E, sometimes from me and Edward, sometimes from other soldiers who'd learned to read along the way. She had a mastery of the written word and was determined to read the captain's letter aloud.

"General orders.
"Headquarters 33D U.S.C.T.,
"Late 1st So. Carolina Volunteers,
"Morris Island, S.C., Feb. 9 1866

"Comrades: The hour is at hand when
we must separate forever, and nothing can
take from us the pride we feel, when we
look upon the history of the 'First South
Carolina Volunteers,' the first Black
regiment that ever bore arms in defense of
freedom on the continent of America.
    "On the ninth day of May, 1862, at
which time there were nearly four million
of your race in bondage, sanctioned by
the laws of the land and protected by our
flag—on that day, in the face of the floods
of prejudice that well-nigh deluged every
avenue to manhood and true liberty, you

came forth to do battle for your country and
kindred.

"For long and weary months,
without pay or even the privilege of being
recognized as soldiers, you labored on, only
to be disbanded and sent to your homes
without even a hope of reward, and when
our country, necessitated by the deadly
struggle with armed traitors, finally granted
you the opportunity again to come forth
in defense of the nation's life, the alacrity
with which you responded to the call gave
abundant evidence of your readiness to
strike a manly blow for the liberty of your
race. And from that little band of hopeful,
trusting, and brave men who gathered at
Camp Saxton, on Port Royal Island, in the
fall of '62, amidst the terrible prejudices
that surrounded us, has grown an army of a
hundred and forty thousand Black soldiers,
whose valor and heroism has won for your
race a name which will live as long as
the undying pages of history shall endure;
and by whose efforts, united with those of
the white man, armed rebellion has been
conquered, the millions of bondsmen have
been emancipated, and the fundamental law

of the land has been so altered as to remove
forever the possibility of human slavery
being established within the borders of
redeemed America. The flag of our fathers,
restored to its rightful significance, now
floats over every foot of our territory, from
Maine to California, and beholds only free
men! The prejudices which formerly existed
against you are well-nigh rooted out."

Mary lowered the page and barked out a mirthless laugh. "Only free *men*, he says. And what about us women?"

I shook my head, grumbling under my breath. As much as I admired the colonel, I too was annoyed by all the attention he'd paid to *men* without any mention of the women who'd helped the cause. I remembered a conversation I'd had with Mrs. Beasley in her parlor many years ago. I'd sat in her classroom and asked her: If the Union freed all men, would that include women too? I wanted to vote, wanted to participate.

Now I knew the answer to that question. We would not enjoy the same freedoms as men. And I wondered if Black men would really be able to participate in all aspects of their freedom.

I'd believe it when I saw my husband casting ballots during elections.

Colonel Trowbridge's letter went on to talk about how we'd won our freedom. True, we had fought tooth and nail for our freedom. But the unfairness of having to fight for something so intrinsic to humanity struck me hard. White people didn't have to fight for their rights. It was assumed. It was their birthright.

But even with all that, I'd take my freedom any way I could get it.

The war was over. My service to the Union Army was at an end.

Mary finished reading the colonel's lengthy discharge papers, and we both sank down to sit on the sandy ground. I leaned back and looked at the shapes the clouds made as they drifted across the sky.

"My husband said we'll head out in the morning," I said. "Nothing left for us here in camp."

"Do you think we'll get paid for our service?" Mary looked up from her flowers, a sly smirk creeping across her lips. We both erupted in laughter. It wasn't until 1864 that the government had finally agreed to equal pay for the Colored Troops. But we women, we knew we would never see a dime for our service. Mary's laugh waned to a sigh, then her voice grew quite small. "Where will you go when you leave tomorrow?"

"I'd love to see my family, check and see if they're okay." It had been years since I'd felt my mama's embrace, since I'd heard my grandma humming near her stove. I hadn't heard from either of them since running away from Grest Farm, nor had I received word from my brothers and sisters. The silence was killing me—I had to find out how they'd fared during the war. Only then would I feel comfortable establishing a new home with Edward. I squared my shoulders and lifted my chin. "And after I do that—I've always wanted to start a school."

"That is perfect for you. You were a good teacher and taught me to read. I'll never be able to thank you enough."

"The privilege was all mine."

Epilogue

{ *February 1902* }

J UST ONE TICKET, PLEASE." I REACHED THROUGH
the window to retrieve my boarding pass. My gloved
fingers grazed the clerk's hand as I took the ticket,
which read BOSTON TO CINCINNATI. "Thank you, sir."

"Will you be needing help with your bags today, ma'am?"
His eager eyes craned over the counter in search of my luggage.

"That won't be necessary, thank you." I lifted my small
leather bag, demonstrating how light I was traveling. He
tipped his hat in response, then directed his attentions to the
next customer.

I walked briskly toward the train platform, thankful to
be traveling lightly. It allowed me to move quickly, and I
needed to move quickly if I wanted to catch the last train out
to Cincinnati. It was the only route that allowed me to make
my connections to Louisiana.

My boots clacked against the concrete as I hurried through the double doors and rushed down the stairs. I caught a few reproachful looks—not because of the color of my skin, but because I was a woman traveling alone, who was nearly breaking into a jog. But I didn't care—I didn't have much time to see my son before it was too late.

I reached the platform just as the train light shone on the horizon. It blared its horn as it lugged up the tracks, kicking up a dusty wind that nearly blew my hat off my head. I dug the hatpin deeper into my hair, securing it to weather the journey ahead.

In truth, I wouldn't be going back down South if it wasn't for my son. He was the last living piece of my late husband, Edward King. Our time together after the war was short, and I often wondered how different things could've been. We returned to Savannah in 1866 and were immediately reminded that the war was over, but prejudice was not. We were told that we couldn't ride alongside white passengers on boats in Georgia, and I'd steadied myself for life in a post-war South.

Reuniting with Grandma brought a peace of mind I hadn't known for four years. She was healthy and, unsurprisingly, was still finding a way to support herself and squirrel away her money. She was my inspiration, a reminder that I could earn a good living by returning to the thing that I loved most—teaching.

I opened a school at my home on South Broad Street, now

called Oglethorpe Avenue, prepared to do what I had done during my time at camp—teach Black children how to read and write. I had twenty students, and I taught these young scholars for nearly a year. Eventually the Beach Institute, another school, opened its doors. The Beach Institute offered a free education, and I simply couldn't compete. It broke my heart, but I had to close my school. As disappointing as that loss was, nothing compared to the loss of my Edward. He left this world on September 16, 1866, and my only solace was that I was carrying his child. I would name him after his father, a symbol of the love that I would carry in my heart for the rest of my life.

Life was difficult following the loss of my husband. I moved back to Liberty County, Georgia, not far from Grest Farm, and opened another school. But I missed Savannah and decided to return to the city. I taught for a bit, but I needed to find a stable and secure way to provide for my son, so I returned to the work that Black women knew too well—I started cooking and cleaning for white families. For most of us, this was the only kind of work that was available. Many formerly enslaved women moved from slavery into a very similar kind of situation. According to the law we were free people, but it sure didn't feel that way.

My mama watched little Edward as I lived and traveled with families to Boston. Eventually I returned to Georgia, and in 1879 I married my second husband, Russell L. Taylor. We returned north and made a nice life for ourselves in Boston. He worked down by the docks as a longshoreman, and we rented a large home in the city, providing rooms for lodgers. I rebuilt my life and helped organize Corps 67 of the Women's Relief Corps, which helped support our war veterans. I never turned my back on the men who had given so much to the Union cause. In some ways, I did this work in memory of my Edward.

Then in February of 1898, I received the news that no mother ever wants to hear. I learned I was going to lose my son.

The pain was almost too much to bear.

He'd fallen gravely ill while traveling as a performer and ventriloquist with Nickens and Company, acting in their production of *The Lion's Bride*. I tried to bring him home to Boston, but he was not able to sit and ride for such a long distance. A Black man could not be guaranteed a sleeping compartment on a train, so I decided to go to him.

When the train came to a complete stop, its doors flew open, and porters dismounted onto the platform. One of them held his hand out for me to steady myself as I stepped into the car. I chose a seat next to a window and slumped into my chair, catching my breath while another porter loaded my bag in a nearby compartment.

Soon the train eased out of the station, creeping by sleepy Boston neighborhoods, picking up speed as we reached its outlying counties. I'd been to many states and cities, and in each I looked for liberty and justice, equality for all people. But it was not until I was within the borders of New England and reached old Massachusetts that I'd found it. I found liberty in the full sense of the word: liberty for the stranger within her gates, irrespective of race or creed—liberty and justice for all.

I got a pang of early homesickness as I watched Massachusetts whiz past me through the window.

When I reached Cincinnati, I needed to board the train headed south. The station here was different from the one in Boston, with intricate interchanges and a maze of stairs. I was out of breath by the time I made it to the right place. The train was almost finished boarding when I arrived.

"Excuse me, sir!" I waved at a man standing nearby. "Could you tell me what car I should take?"

"Take that one," he said, pointing to the car near the front of the train.

"But that one is a smoking car." I squinted at the long train, at all the empty seats I could see through the windows. My ticket didn't say anything about being seated in the smoking section. "Surely there is another option."

"Well," he said, his eyes tightening. He looked at me like I was a foreigner in a strange land. "It don't really matter what your ticket says. You sit where I tell you to sit—with the rest of your kind."

His words hit me like a ton of bricks. I was no longer in Boston. I was in the beginning of what folks were starting to call the Jim Crow South, a system that kept Blacks and whites separate and unequal.

I walked to the car at the front of the train. There was no

porter to lend me a helping hand, so I tossed my leather bag
onto the train before hoisting myself up the steps. The aisle
was cramped with people and bags. The smell of coal, stale
smoke, and musty upholstery hung heavy in the air.

All my courage failed me. I'd ridden in many coaches,
but never in one like this. I wanted to return home again, but
when I thought of my dying baby boy, I said to myself, "Others
ride in these cars, and I must do likewise."

I tried to make the best of it, but it sure was hard to see
the positive side of things.

I arrived in Chattanooga, Tennessee, at eight o'clock in the
evening, and the porter took my baggage to the train, which
was to leave for Marion, Mississippi. Soon after I found my
seat, and just before the train pulled out, two tall men with
slouch hats walked through the car, eyeing the passengers
suspiciously. They weren't dressed for travel, and they didn't
have any bags or tickets in sight. If there was anything suspicious on the train, it was them. They stopped at my seat.

"Where are those men who were with you?"

"Are you speaking to me?" I looked around the car. There
was another woman seated a few rows ahead of me. Perhaps
they were speaking to her.

"Yes!" the men said in unison. The one with the mustache
stepped forward and stood directly in front of my seat. He
scowled at me and asked, "Where are those men who came
in with you?"

"I haven't seen any men." I shook my head and averted my eyes, instantly feeling as though I'd been transported back to my time on Grest Farm before the war.

"Where are you from?" The mustache man leaned forward. He was so close, I could smell the tobacco smoke on his whiskers—definitely too close for comfort.

I wanted to tell them that it was none of their business, but something about the sneers on their faces told me to keep my mouth shut. These men were dangerous.

"I'm from Boston," I said, feeling my pulse quicken.

The men hesitated a minute, then walked out of our car to the next one just as a porter entered the coach.

"Pardon me, sir?" I stood up, shaken and disturbed from the encounter. I pointed to the adjoining car, where I could still see my harassers through the window. "Those men over there were quite rude and aggressive. I'm not even certain they're passengers. Does this rail line allow people to enter the car and insult passengers?"

"Lady, I see you do not belong here," said the porter. He raised his hands and then lowered them slowly, encouraging me to sit down. When I finally sat, he leaned against the top of the neighboring chair, his dark brown eyes wrinkled and weary. "Where are you from?"

"That's exactly what they asked me." I crossed my arms, still upset. "I'm from Boston."

"I have often heard of Massachusetts." He sighed heavily. "I want to see that place."

"You can ride there on the cars, and no person would be allowed to speak to you as those men did to me."

"Those men were constables in search of a man who had eloped with another man's wife, or so they claim." He shrugged, shaking his head. "That is the way they do us here. Every morning, I hear of some poor fellow being lynched."

"I don't understand. How can they do that?"

"Oh, that's nothing. It's done all the time. We have no rights here." He ran his fingers through his coarse curls. "I have been on this rail line for fifteen years and have seen some terrible things. If I were you, I'd head back to Boston as quick as I could."

He shoved off the seat, and with a tap of his porter's cap, he sidled down the aisle and opened the door to the next compartment. I huddled closer to the window, making myself as small and unobtrusive as possible. My breath hitched, and a tear ran down the side of my face.

For the first time in a long while, I was scared because of the color of my skin.

The train lurched forward, finally departing from the Chattanooga station. The rude constables glared up at the windows from the platform as my car swept by them.

"Good riddance," I said under my breath. The woman sitting a few rows in front of me looked at me out of the side of her eye, but she had the grace to give me my privacy. I was glad to leave those dangerous men behind. But I still couldn't shake my fear. It took root in my belly, like a stomachache I couldn't shake.

I wanted to get out of Tennessee as soon as possible. I knew that the United Daughters of the Confederacy was busy in these parts, trying to rewrite history by honoring their ancestors who had worn gray Confederate uniforms and fought against our nation. They petitioned managers of local theaters across the state to prohibit any performances based on the book *Uncle Tom's Cabin*. They said that the play was untruthful and that it depicted slavery in exaggerated ways. They claimed they wanted to prevent children from seeing the production because it might have a bad effect on them.

How absurd.

I'd witnessed truly horrible things in my childhood that could harm children. The memory that still haunts me is of the countless people I watched marching down my street in shackles. Every first Tuesday of each month, dozens of men, women, and children were marched from Mr. Wiley's trade office to the auction block, where they were sold to the highest bidder.

The route the enslavers used passed right in front of my grandmother's house in Savannah. Only a block away from us, I could hear the auctioneer very plainly from my house, selling these poor people off. I am forever haunted by this.

I could also still remember my days in Savannah, where lynchings were now a common occurrence. I still felt the fear of my ancestors, who for two hundred years had tilled and toiled the ground beneath my feet, and who endured horrific abuse. It was a deep-seated fear I'd hoped to never feel again.

I had prayed that my son, who was born a free man, would never feel this way.

But his work took him on travels around the country, including the South. And here, there was no avoiding that fear.

Did these Daughters of the Confederacy ever send petitions to prohibit the atrocious lynchings of Black people? I'd never heard of them claiming a noose could have a bad effect on the children. But they protested books and performances. Which of these two realities made a degrading impression upon the minds of our young generation—a play or a brutal hanging?

Education was always my key to unlocking understanding. And the knowledge I'd gained was truly empowering. What children needed now was more education about the past, more instruction on how to live in harmony, and more reverence for our country's history, so that we didn't repeat the mistakes of the past. If I were still a teacher, that's where I would focus my pupils' attention.

But I couldn't live out my dream of being a teacher. As a Black woman living in Georgia after the war, my options were limited and my dreams were out of reach. And now the South was backsliding into pervasive fear again. That made me shudder.

When the war ended, I'd hoped my race was forever free from bondage, that the two races could live in unity with each other. But with lynchings every day, the Ku Klux Klan on the rise, segregation as the law of the land, and palpable fear pumping through our veins—I wasn't sure if we had accomplished freedom and justice.

The train continued south as I thought.

Was the war in vain?

My family was still struggling to survive in a system built to keep us down. My grandmother, who had saved every penny she'd earned from laundering clothes and cleaning bachelors' rooms, was finding it hard to make ends meet after the Freedman's Savings Bank had failed. And now my son lay dying in the segregated South.

This country was deeply flawed, and I wasn't certain I'd live to see the day when it repented for the blood of innocents it had shed.

But I still believed in a more perfect union. Even as I traveled back into the deep South, I had to believe it was an attainable dream. The United States had made progress through the abolition of slavery. As I continued on my journey, I would keep working tirelessly for our just cause, so that the stars and stripes would never be polluted again.

The following is the text that Susie King Taylor wrote and published in 1902. We feel it is important not only to know her story but also read her own words.

—E. A. B. and C. B.

REMINISCENCES OF MY LIFE IN CAMP

WITH THE 33D UNITED STATES
COLORED TROOPS LATE 1ST
S. C. VOLUNTEERS

BY

SUSIE KING TAYLOR

BOSTON
PUBLISHED BY THE AUTHOR
1902

To

COLONEL T. W. HIGGINSON

THESE PAGES
ARE GRATEFULLY DEDICATED

PREFACE

I HAVE BEEN ASKED MANY TIMES BY MY friends, and also by members of the Grand Army of the Republic and Women's Relief Corps, to write a book of my army life, during the war of 1861–65, with the regiment of the 1st South Carolina Colored Troops, later called 33d United States Colored Infantry.

At first I did not think I would, but as the years rolled on and my friends were still urging me to start with it, I wrote to Colonel C. T. Trowbridge (who had command of this regiment), asking his opinion and advice on the matter. His answer to me was, "Go ahead! Write it; that is just what I should do, were I in your place, and I will give you all the assistance you may need, whenever you require it." This inspired me very much.

In 1900 I received a letter from a gentleman, sent from

the Executive Mansion at St. Paul, Minn., saying Colonel Trowbridge had told him I was about to write a book, and when it was published he wanted one of the first copies. This, coming from a total stranger, gave me more confidence, so I now present these reminiscences to you, hoping they may prove of some interest, and show how much service and good we can do to each other, and what sacrifices we can make for our liberty and rights, and that there were "loyal women," as well as men, in those days, who did not fear shell or shot, who cared for the sick and dying; women who camped and fared as the boys did, and who are still caring for the comrades in their declining years.

So, with the hope that the following pages will accomplish some good and instruction for its readers, I shall proceed with my narrative.

SUSIE KING TAYLOR.

BOSTON, 1902.

CONTENTS

INTRODUCTION

ACTUAL MILITARY LIFE IS RARELY described by a woman, and this is especially true of a woman whose place was in the ranks, as the wife of a soldier and herself a regimental laundress. No such description has ever been given, I am sure, by one thus connected with a colored regiment; so that the nearly 200,000 black soldiers (178,975) of our Civil War have never before been delineated from the woman's point of view. All this gives peculiar interest to this little volume, relating wholly to the career of the very earliest of these regiments—the one described by myself, from a wholly different point of view, in my volume "Army Life in a Black Regiment," long since translated into French by the Comtesse de Gasparin under the title "Vie Militaire dans un Régiment Noir."

The writer of the present book was very exceptional

among the colored laundresses, in that she could read and write and had taught children to do the same; and her whole life and career were most estimable, both during the war and in the later period during which she has lived in Boston and has made many friends. I may add that I did not see the book until the sheets were in print, and have left it wholly untouched, except as to a few errors in proper names. I commend the narrative to those who love the plain record of simple lives, led in stormy periods.

THOMAS WENTWORTH HIGGINSON,
Former Colonel 1st S. C. Volunteers
(afterwards 38d U. S. Colored Infantry).

LETTER FROM COL. C. T. TROWBRIDGE

ST. PAUL, MINN., April 7, 1902.
MRS. SUSAN KING TAYLOR:

DEAR MADAM—THE MANUSCRIPT OF the story of your army life reached me today. I have read it with much care and interest, and I most willingly and cordially indorse it as a truthful account of your unselfish devotion and service through more than three long years of war in which the 33d Regiment bore a conspicuous part in the great conflict for human liberty and the restoration of the Union. I most sincerely regret that through a technicality you are debarred from having your name placed on the roll of pensioners, as an Army Nurse; for among all the number of heroic women whom the government is now rewarding, I know of no one more deserving than yourself.

Yours in F. C. & L.,
C. T. TROWBRIDGE,
Late Lt.-Col. 33d U. S. C. T.

REMINISCENCES

I

A BRIEF SKETCH
OF MY ANCESTORS

MY GREAT-GREAT-GRANDMOTHER WAS 120 years old when she died. She had seven children, and five of her boys were in the Revolutionary War. She was from Virginia, and was half Indian. She was so old she had to be held in the sun to help restore or prolong her vitality.

My great-grandmother, one of her daughters, named Susanna, was married to Peter Simons, and was one hundred years old when she died, from a stroke of paralysis in Savannah. She was the mother of twenty-four children, twenty-three being girls. She was one of the noted midwives of her day. In 1820 my grandmother was born, and named after her grandmother, Dolly, and in 1833 she married Fortune Lambert Reed. Two children blessed their union, James and Hagar Ann. James died at the age of twelve years.

My mother was born in 1834. She married Raymond Baker in 1847. Nine children were born to them, three dying in infancy. I was the first born. I was born on the Grest Farm (which was on an island known as Isle of Wight), Liberty County, about thirty-five miles from Savannah, Ga., on August 6, 1848, my mother being waitress for the Grest family. I have often been told by mother of the care Mrs. Grest took of me. She was very fond of me, and I remember when my brother and I were small children, and Mr. Grest would go away on business, Mrs. Grest would place us at the foot of her bed to sleep and keep her company. Sometimes he would return home earlier than he had expected to; then she would put us on the floor.

When I was about seven years old, Mr. Grest allowed my grandmother to take my brother and me to live with her in Savannah. There were no railroad connections in those days between this place and Savannah; all travel was by stagecoaches. I remember, as if it were yesterday, the coach which ran in from Savannah, with its driver, whose beard nearly reached his knees. His name was Shakespeare, and often I would go to the stable where he kept his horses, on Barnard Street in front of the old Arsenal, just to look at his wonderful beard.

My grandmother went every three months to see my mother. She would hire a wagon to carry bacon, tobacco, flour, molasses, and sugar. These she would trade with people in the neighboring places, for eggs, chickens, or cash, if they had it. These, in turn, she carried back to the city market, where she had a customer who sold them for her. The profit from these, together with laundry work and care of some bachelors' rooms, made a good living for her.

The hardest blow to her was the failure of the Freedman's Savings Bank in Savannah, for in that bank she had placed her savings, about three thousand dollars, the result of her hard labor and self-denial before the war, and which, by dint of shrewdness and care, she kept together all through the war. She felt it more keenly, coming as it did in her old age, when her life was too far spent to begin anew; but she took a practical view of the matter, for she said, "I will leave it all in God's hand. If the Yankees did take all our money, they freed my race; God will take care of us."

In 1888 she wrote me here (Boston), asking me to visit her, as she was getting very feeble and wanted to see me once before she passed away. I made up my mind to leave at once, but about the time I planned to go, in March, a fearful blizzard swept our country, and travel was at a standstill for nearly two weeks; but March 15 I left on the first through steamer from New York, en route for the South, where I again saw my grandmother, and we felt thankful that we were spared to meet each other once more. This was the last time I saw her, for in May, 1889, she died.

II

MY CHILDHOOD

I WAS BORN UNDER THE SLAVE LAW IN Georgia, in 1848, and was brought up by my grandmother in Savannah. There were three of us with her, my younger sister and brother. My brother and I being the two eldest, we were sent to a friend of my grandmother, Mrs. Woodhouse, a widow, to learn to read and write. She was a free woman and lived on Bay Lane, between Habersham and Price streets, about half a mile from my house. We went every day about nine o'clock, with our books wrapped in paper to prevent the police or white persons from seeing them. We went in, one at a time, through the gate, into the yard to the L kitchen, which was the schoolroom. She had twenty-five or thirty children whom she taught, assisted by her daughter, Mary Jane. The neighbors would see us going in sometimes, but they supposed we were there learning trades, as it was the custom to give children a trade of some kind. After school we left the same way we entered, one by one, when we would go to a square, about a block from the school, and wait for each other. We would gather laurel leaves and pop them on our hands, on our way home. I remained at her school for two years or more, when I was sent to a Mrs. Mary Beasley, where I continued until May, 1860, when she told my grandmother she had taught me all she knew, and grandmother had better get some one else who could teach me more, so I stopped my studies for a while.

I had a white playmate about this time, named Katie O'Connor, who lived on the next corner of the street from my house, and who attended a convent. One day she told me, if I would promise not to tell her father, she would give me some lessons. On my promise not to do so, and getting her mother's consent, she gave me lessons about four months, every evening. At the end of this time she was put into the convent permanently, and I have never seen her since.

A month after this, James Blouis, our landlord's son, was attending the High School, and was very fond of grandmother, so she asked him to give me a few lessons, which he did until the middle of 1861, when the Savannah Volunteer Guards, to which he and his brother belonged, were ordered to the front under General Barton. In the first battle of Manassas, his brother Eugene was killed, and James deserted over to the Union side, and at the close of the war went to Washington, D. C., where he has since resided.

I often wrote passes for my grandmother, for all colored persons, free or slaves, were compelled to have a pass; free colored people having a guardian in place of a master. These passes were good until 10 or 10.30 P. M. for one night or every night for one month. The pass read as follows:

SAVANNAH, GA., March 1st, 1860.
Pass the bearer——from 9 to 10.30. P. M.
VALENTINE GREST.

Every person had to have this pass, for at nine o'clock each night a bell was rung, and any colored persons found on the street after this hour were arrested by the watchman, and put in the guard-house until next morning, when their owners would pay their fines and release them. I knew a number of persons who went out at any time at night and were never arrested, as the watchman knew them so well he never stopped them, and seldom asked to see their passes, only stopping them long enough, sometimes, to say "Howdy," and then telling them to go along.

About this time I had been reading so much about the "Yankees" I was very anxious to see them. The whites would tell their colored people not to go to the Yankees, for they would harness them to carts and make them pull the carts around, in place of horses. I asked grandmother, one day, if this was true. She replied, "Certainly not!" that the white people did not want slaves to go over to the Yankees, and told them these things to frighten them. "Don't you see those signs pasted about the streets? One reading, 'I am a rattlesnake; if you touch me I will strike!' Another reads, 'I am a wild-cat! Beware,' etc. These are warnings to the North; so don't mind what the white people say." I wanted to see these wonderful "Yankees" so much, as I heard my parents say the Yankee was going to set all the slaves free. Oh, how those people prayed for freedom! I remember, one night, my grandmother went out into the suburbs of the city to a church meeting, and they were fervently singing this old hymn—

> *"Yes, we all shall be free,*
> *Yes, we all shall be free,*
> *Yes, we all shall be free,*
> *When the Lord shall appear—"*

when the police came in and arrested all who were there, saying they were planning freedom, and sang "the Lord," in place of "Yankee," to blind any one who might be listening. Grandmother never forgot that night, although she did not stay in the guard-house, as she sent to her guardian, who came at once for her; but this was the last meeting she ever attended out of the city proper.

On April 1, 1862, about the time the Union soldiers were firing on Fort Pulaski, I was sent out into the country to my mother. I remember what a roar and din the guns made. They jarred the earth for miles. The fort was at last taken by them.

Two days after the taking of Fort Pulaski, my uncle took his family of seven and myself to St. Catherines Island. We landed under the protection of the Union fleet, and remained there two weeks, when about thirty of us were taken aboard the gunboat P——, to be transferred to St. Simons Island; and at last, to my unbounded joy, I saw the "Yankee."

After we were all settled aboard and started on our journey, Captain Whitmore, commanding the boat, asked me where I was from. I told him Savannah, Ga. He asked if I could read; I said, "Yes!" "Can you write?" he next asked. "Yes, I can do that also," I replied, and as if he had some doubts of my answers he handed me a book and a pencil and told me to write my name and where I was from. I did this; then he wanted to know if I could sew. On hearing I could, he asked me to hem some napkins for him. He was surprised at my accomplishments (for they were such in those days), for he said he did not know there were any negroes in the South able to read or write. He said, "You seem to be so different from the other colored people who came from the same place you did." "No!" I replied, "the only difference is, they were reared in the country and I in the city, as was a man from Darien, Ga., named Edward King." That seemed to satisfy him, and we had no further conversation that day on the subject.

In the afternoon the captain spied a boat in the distance, and as it drew nearer he noticed it had a white flag hoisted, but before it had reached the *Putumoka* he ordered all passengers between decks, so we could not be seen, for he thought they might be spies. The boat finally drew alongside of our boat, and had Mr. Edward Donegall on board, who wanted his two servants, Nick and Judith. He wanted these, as they were his own children. Our captain told him he knew nothing of them, which was true, for at the time they were on St. Simons, and not, as their father supposed, on our boat. After the boat left, we were allowed to come up on deck again.

III

ON ST. SIMONS ISLAND

{ *1862* }

NEXT MORNING WE ARRIVED AT ST. Simons, and the captain told Commodore Goldsborough about this affair, and his reply was, "Captain Whitmore, you should not have allowed them to return; you should have kept them." After I had been on St. Simons about three days, Commodore Goldsborough heard of me, and came to Gaston Bluff to see me. I found him very cordial. He said Captain Whitmore had spoken to him of me, and that he was pleased to hear of my being so capable, etc., and wished me to take charge of a school for the children on the island. I told him I would gladly do so, if I could have some books. He said I should have them, and in a week or two I received two large boxes of books and testaments from the North. I had about forty children to teach, beside a number of adults who came to me nights, all of them so eager to learn to read, to read above anything else. Chaplain French, of Boston, would come to the school, sometimes, and lecture to the pupils on Boston and the North.

About the first of June we were told that there was going to be a settlement of the war. Those who were on the Union side would remain free, and those in bondage were to work three days for their masters and three for themselves. It was a gloomy time for us all, and we were to be sent to Liberia. Chaplain French asked me would I rather go back to Savannah or go to Liberia. I told him the latter place by all means. We did not know when this would be, but we were prepared in case this settlement should be reached. However, the Confederates would not agree to the arrangement, or else it was one of the many rumors flying about at the time, as we heard nothing further of the matter. There were a number of settlements on this island of St. Simons, just like little villages, and we would go from one to the other on business, to call, or only for a walk.

One Sunday, two men, Adam Miller and Daniel Spaulding, were chased by some rebels as they were coming from Hope Place (which was between the Beach and Gaston Bluff), but the latter were unable to catch them. When they reached the Beach and told this, all the men on the place, about ninety, armed themselves, and next day (Monday), with Charles O'Neal as their leader, skirmished the island for the "rebs." In a short while they discovered them in the woods, hidden behind a large log, among the thick underbrush. Charles

O'Neal was the first to see them, and he was killed; also John Brown, and their bodies were never found. Charles O'Neal was an uncle of Edward King, who later was my husband and a sergeant in Co. E., U. S. I. Another man was shot, but not found for three days. On Tuesday, the second day, Captain Trowbridge and some soldiers landed, and assisted the skirmishers. Word having been sent by the mail-boat *Uncas* to Hilton Head, later in the day Commodore Goldsborough, who was in command of the naval station, landed about three hundred marines, and joined the others to oust the rebels. On Wednesday, John Baker, the man shot on Monday, was found in a terrible condition by Henry Batchlott, who carried him to the Beach, where he was attended by the surgeon. He told us how, after being shot, he lay quiet for a day. On the second day he managed to reach some wild grapes growing near him. These he ate, to satisfy his hunger and intense thirst, then he crawled slowly, every movement causing agony, until he got to the side of the road. He lived only three months after they found him.

On the second day of the skirmish the troops captured a boat which they knew the Confederates had used to land in, and having this in their possession, the "rebs" could not return; so pickets were stationed all around the island. There was an old man, Henry Capers, who had been left on one of the places by his old master, Mr. Hazzard, as he was too old to carry away. These rebels went to his house in the night, and he hid them up in the loft. On Tuesday all hands went to this man's house with a determination to burn it down, but Henry Batchlott pleaded with the men to spare it. The rebels were in hiding, still, waiting a chance to get off the island. They searched his house, but neglected to go up into the loft, and in so doing missed the rebels concealed there. Late in the night Henry Capers gave them his boat to escape in, and they got off all right. This old man was allowed by the men in charge of the island to cut grass for his horse, and to have a boat to carry this grass to his home, and so they were not detected, our men thinking it was Capers using the boat. After Commodore Goldsborough left the island, Commodore Judon sent the old man over to the mainland and would not allow him to remain on the island.

There were about six hundred men, women, and children on St. Simons, the women and children being in the majority, and we were afraid to go very far from our own quarters in the daytime, and at night even to go out of the house for a long time, although the men were on the watch all the time; for there were not any soldiers on the island, only the marines who were on the gunboats along the coast. The rebels, knowing this, could steal by them under cover of the night, and getting on the island would capture any persons venturing out alone and carry them to the mainland. Several of the men disappeared, and as they were never heard from we came to the conclusion they had been carried off in this way.

The latter part of August, 1862, Captain C. T. Trowbridge, with his brother John and Lieutenant Walker, came to St.

Simons Island from Hilton Head, by order of General Hunter, to get all the men possible to finish filling his regiment which he had organized in March, 1862. He had heard of the skirmish on this island, and was very much pleased at the bravery shown by these men. He found me at Gaston Bluff teaching my little school, and was much interested in it. When I knew him better I found him to be a thorough gentleman and a staunch friend to my race.

Captain Trowbridge remained with us until October, when the order was received to evacuate, and so we boarded the *Ben-De-Ford*, a transport, for Beaufort, S. C. When we arrived in Beaufort, Captain Trowbridge and the men he had enlisted went to camp at Old Fort, which they named "Camp Saxton." I was enrolled as laundress.

The first suits worn by the boys were red coats and pants, which they disliked very much, for, they said, "The rebels see us, miles away."

The first colored troops did not receive any pay for eighteen months, and the men had to depend wholly on what they received from the commissary, established by General Saxton. A great many of these men had large families, and as they had no money to give them, their wives were obliged to support themselves and children by washing for the officers of the gunboats and the soldiers, and making cakes and pies which they sold to the boys in camp. Finally, in 1863, the government decided to give them half pay, but the men would not accept this. They wanted "full pay" or nothing. They preferred rather to give their services to the state, which they did until 1864, when the government granted them full pay, with all the back pay due.

I remember hearing Captain Heasley telling his company, one day, "Boys, stand up for your full pay! I am with you, and so are all the officers." This captain was from Pennsylvania, and was a very good man; all the men liked him. N. G. Parker, our first lieutenant, was from Massachusetts. H. A. Beach was from New York. He was very delicate, and had to resign in 1864 on account of ill health.

I had a number of relatives in this regiment—several uncles, some cousins, and a husband in Company E, and a number of cousins in other companies. Major Strong, of this regiment, started home on a furlough, but the vessel he was aboard was lost, and he never reached his home. He was one of the best officers we had. After his death, Captain C. T. Trowbridge was promoted major, August, 1863, and filled Major Strong's place until December, 1864, when he was promoted lieutenant-colonel, which he remained until he was mustered out, February 6, 1866.

In February, 1863, several cases of varioloid broke out among the boys, which caused some anxiety in camp. Edward Davis, of Company E (the company I was with), had it very badly. He was put into a tent apart from the rest of the men, and only the doctor and camp steward, James Cummings, were allowed to see or attend him; but I went to see this man every day and nursed him. The last thing at night, I always went in to see that he was comfortable, but in spite of the good care and attention he received, he succumbed to the disease.

I was not in the least afraid of the smallpox. I had been vaccinated, and I drank sassafras tea constantly, which kept my blood purged and prevented me from contracting this dread scourge, and no one need fear getting it if they will only keep their blood in good condition with this sassafras tea, and take it before going where the patient is.

IV

CAMP SAXTON–
PROCLAMATION
AND BARBECUE

{ 1863 }

O N THE FIRST OF JANUARY, 1863, WE
held services for the purpose of listening to the
reading of President Lincoln's proclamation by
Dr. W. H. Brisbane, and the presentation of two beautiful
stands of colors, one from a lady in Connecticut, and the
other from Rev. Mr. Cheever. The presentation speech was
made by Chaplain French. It was a glorious day for us all, and
we enjoyed every minute of it, and as a fitting close and the
crowning event of this occasion we had a grand barbecue. A
number of oxen were roasted whole, and we had a fine feast.
Although not served as tastily or correctly as it would have
been at home, yet it was enjoyed with keen appetites and rel-
ish. The soldiers had a good time. They sang or shouted "Hurrah!" all through the camp, and seemed overflowing with fun

and frolic until taps were sounded, when many, no doubt, dreamt of this memorable day.

I had rather an amusing experience; that is, it seems amusing now, as I look back, but at the time it occurred it was a most serious one to me. When our regiment left Beaufort for Seabrooke, I left some of my things with a neighbor who lived outside of the camp. After I had been at Seabrooke about a week, I decided to return to Camp Saxton and get them. So one morning, with Mary Shaw, a friend who was in the company at that time, I started off. There was no way for us to get to Beaufort other than to walk, except we rode on the commissary wagon. This we did, and reached Beaufort about one o'clock. We then had more than two miles to walk before reaching our old camp, and expected to be able to accomplish this and return in time to meet the wagon again by three o'clock that afternoon, and so be taken back. We failed to do this, however, for when we got to Beaufort the wagon was gone. We did not know what to do. I did not wish to remain overnight; neither did my friend, although we might easily have stayed, as both had relatives in the town.

It was in the springtime, and the days were long, and as the sun looked so bright, we concluded to walk back, thinking we should reach camp before dark. So off we started on our ten-mile tramp. We had not gone many miles, however, before we were all tired out and began to regret our undertaking. The sun was getting low, and we grew more frightened, fearful of meeting some animal or of treading on a snake on our way. We did not meet a person, and we were frightened almost to death. Our feet were so sore we could hardly walk. Finally we took off our shoes and tried walking in our stocking feet, but this made them worse. We had gone about six miles when night overtook us. There we were, nothing around us but dense woods, and as there was no house or any place to stop at, there was nothing for us to do but continue on. We were afraid to speak to each other.

Meantime at the camp, seeing no signs of us by dusk, they concluded we had decided to remain over until next day, and so had no idea of our plight. Imagine their surprise when we reached camp about eleven p.m. The guard challenged us, "Who comes there?" My answer was, "A friend without a countersign." He approached and saw who it was, reported, and we were admitted into the lines. They had the joke on us that night, and for a long time after would tease us; and sometimes some of the men who were on guard that night would call us deserters. They used to laugh at us, but we joined with them too, especially when we would tell them our experience on our way to camp. I did not undertake that trip again, as there was no way of getting in or out except one took the provision wagon, and there was not much dependence to be put in that returning to camp. Perhaps the driver would say one hour and he might be there earlier or later. Of course it was not his fault, as it depended when the order was filled at the Commissary Department; therefore I did not go any more until the regiment was ordered to our new camp, which was named after our hero, Colonel Shaw, who at that time was at Beaufort with his regiment, the 54th Massachusetts.

I taught a great many of the comrades in Company E to read and write, when they were off duty. Nearly all were anxious to learn. My husband taught some also when it was convenient for him. I was very happy to know my efforts were successful in camp, and also felt grateful for the appreciation of my services. I gave my services willingly for four years and three months without receiving a dollar. I was glad, however, to be allowed to go with the regiment, to care for the sick and afflicted comrades.

V

MILITARY
EXPEDITIONS, AND
LIFE IN CAMP

IN THE LATTER PART OF 1862 THE REGI-
ment made an expedition into Darien, Georgia, and
up the Ridge, and on January 23, 1863, another up St.
Mary's River, capturing a number of stores for the government; then on to Fernandina, Florida. They were gone ten or
twelve days, at the end of which time they returned to camp.

March 10, 1863, we were ordered to Jacksonville, Florida.
Leaving Camp Saxton between four and five o'clock, we
arrived at Jacksonville about eight o'clock next morning,
accompanied by three or four gunboats. When the rebels saw
these boats, they ran out of the city, leaving the women behind,
and we found out afterwards that they thought we had a much
larger fleet than we really had. Our regiment was kept out of
sight until we made fast at the wharf where it landed, and while

the gunboats were shelling up the river and as far inland as possible, the regiment landed and marched up the street, where they spied the rebels who had fled from the city. They were hiding behind a house about a mile or so away, their faces blackened to disguise themselves as negroes, and our boys, as they advanced toward them, halted a second, saying, "They are black men! Let them come to us, or we will make them know who we are." With this, the firing was opened and several of our men were wounded and killed. The rebels had a number wounded and killed. It was through this way the discovery was made that they were white men. Our men drove them some distance in retreat and then threw out their pickets.

While the fighting was on, a friend, Lizzie Lancaster, and I stopped at several of the rebel homes, and after talking with some of the women and children we asked them if they had any food. They claimed to have only some hardtack, and evidently did not care to give us anything to eat, but this was not surprising. They were bitterly against our people and had no mercy or sympathy for us.

The second day, our boys were reinforced by a regiment of white soldiers, a Maine regiment, and by cavalry, and had quite a fight. On the third day, Edward Herron, who was a fine gunner on the steamer *John Adams*, came on shore, bringing a small cannon, which the men pulled along for more than five miles. This cannon was the only piece for shelling. On coming upon the enemy, all secured their places, and they had a lively fight, which lasted several hours, and our boys were nearly captured by the Confederates; but the Union boys carried out all their plans that day, and succeeded in driving the enemy back. After this skirmish, every afternoon between four and five o'clock the Confederate General Finegan would send a flag of truce to Colonel Higginson, warning him to send all women and children out of the city, and threatening to bombard it if this was not done. Our colonel allowed all to go who wished, at first, but as General Finegan grew more hostile and kept sending these communications for nearly a week, Colonel Higginson thought it not best or necessary to send any more out of the city, and so informed General Finegan. This angered the general, for that night the rebels shelled directly toward Colonel Higginson's headquarters. The shelling was so heavy that the colonel told my captain to have me taken up into the town to a hotel, which was used as a hospital. As my quarters were just in the rear of the colonel's, he was compelled to leave his also before the night was over. I expected every moment to be killed by a shell, but on arriving at the hospital I knew I was safe, for the shells could not reach us there. It was plainly to be seen now, the ruse of the flag of truce coming so often to us. The bearer was evidently a spy getting the location of the headquarters, etc., for the shells were sent too accurately to be at random.

Next morning Colonel Higginson took the cavalry and a regiment on another tramp after the rebels. They were gone several days and had the hardest fight they had had, for they wanted to go as far as a station which was some distance from the city. The gunboats were of little assistance to them, yet notwithstanding this drawback our boys returned with only a few killed and wounded, and after this we were not troubled with General Finegan.

We remained here a few weeks longer, when, about April first, the regiment was ordered back to Camp Saxton, where it stayed a week, when the order came to go to Port Royal Ferry on picket duty. It was a gay day for the boys. By seven o'clock all tents were down, and each company, with a commissary wagon, marched up the shell road, which is a beautiful avenue ten or twelve miles out of Beaufort. We arrived at Seabrooke at about four o'clock, where our tents were pitched and the men put on duty. We were here a few weeks, when Company E was ordered to Barnwell plantation for picket duty.

Some mornings I would go along the picket line, and I could see the rebels on the opposite side of the river. Sometimes as they were changing pickets they would call over to our men and ask for something to eat, or for tobacco, and our men would tell them to come over. Sometimes one or two would desert to us, saying, they "had no negroes to fight for." Others would shoot across at our picket, but as the river was so wide there was never any damage done, and the Confederates never attempted to shell us while we were there.

I learned to handle a musket very well while in the regiment, and could shoot straight and often hit the target. I assisted in cleaning the guns and used to fire them off, to see if the cartridges were dry, before cleaning and reloading, each day. I thought this great fun. I was also able to take a gun all apart, and put it together again.

Between Barnwell and the mainland was Hall Island. I went over there several times with Sergeant King and other comrades. One night there was a stir in camp when it was found that the rebels were trying to cross, and next morning Lieutenant Parker told me he thought they were on Hall Island; so after that I did not go over again.

While planning for the expedition up the Edisto River, Colonel Higginson was a whole night in the water, trying to locate the rebels and where their picket lines were situated. About July the boys went up the Edisto to destroy a bridge on the Charleston and Savannah road. This expedition was twenty or more miles into the mainland. Colonel Higginson was wounded in this fight and the regiment nearly captured. The steamboat *John Adams* always assisted us, carrying soldiers, provisions, etc. She carried several guns and a good gunner, Edward Herron. Henry Batchlott, a relative of mine, was a steward on this boat. There were two smaller boats, *Governor Milton* and the *Enoch Dean*, in the fleet, as these could go up the river better than the larger ones could. I often went aboard the *John Adams*. It went with us into Jacksonville, to Cole and Folly Island, and Gunner Herron was always ready to send a shell at the enemy.

One night, Companies K and E, on their way to

Pocotaligo to destroy a battery that was situated down the river, captured several prisoners. The rebels nearly captured Sergeant King, who, as he sprang and caught a "reb," fell over an embankment. In falling he did not release his hold on his prisoner. Although his hip was severely injured, he held fast until some of his comrades came to his aid and pulled them up. These expeditions were very dangerous. Sometimes the men had to go five or ten miles during the night over on the rebel side and capture or destroy whatever they could find.

While at Camp Shaw, there was a deserter who came into Beaufort. He was allowed his freedom about the city and was not molested. He remained about the place a little while and returned to the rebels again. On his return to Beaufort a second time, he was held as a spy, tried, and sentenced to death, for he was a traitor. The day he was shot, he was placed on a hearse with his coffin inside, a guard was placed either side of the hearse, and he was driven through the town. All the soldiers and people in town were out, as this was to be a warning to the soldiers. Our regiment was in line on dress parade. They drove with him to the rear of our camp, where he was shot. I shall never forget this scene.

While at Camp Shaw, Chaplain Fowler, Robert Defoe, and several of our boys were captured while tapping some telegraph wires. Robert Defoe was confined in the jail at Walterborough, S. C., for about twenty months. When Sherman's army reached Pocotaligo he made his escape and joined his company (Company G). He had not been paid, as he had refused the reduced pay offered by the government. Before we got to camp, where the payrolls could be made out, he sickened and died of smallpox, and was buried at Savannah, never having been paid one cent for nearly three years of service. He left no heirs and his account was never settled.

In winter, when it was very cold, I would take a mess pan, put a little earth in the bottom, and go to the cook shed and fill it nearly full of coals, carry it back to my tent and put another pan over it; so when the provost guard went through camp after taps, they would not see the light, as it was against the rules to have a light after taps. In this way I was heated and kept very warm.

A mess pan is made of sheet iron, something like our roasting pans, only they are nearly as large round as a peck measure, but not so deep. We had fresh beef once in a while, and we would have soup, and the vegetables they put in this soup were dried and pressed. They looked like hops. Salt beef was our standby. Sometimes the men would have what we called slap-jacks. This was flour, made into bread and spread thin on the bottom of the mess pan to cook. Each man had one of them, with a pint of tea, for his supper, or a pint of tea and five or six hardtack. I often got my own meals, and would fix some dishes for the non-commissioned officers also.

Mrs. Chamberlain, our quartermaster's wife, was with us here. She was a beautiful woman; I can see her pleasant face before me now, as she, with Captain Trowbridge, would sit and converse with me in my tent two or three hours at a time. She was also with me on Cole Island, and I think we were the only women with the regiment while there. I remember well how, when she first came into camp, Captain Trowbridge brought her to my tent and introduced her to me. I found her then, as she remained ever after, a lovely person, and I always admired her cordial and friendly ways.

Our boys would say to me sometimes, "Mrs. King, why is it you are so kind to us? You treat us just as you do the boys in your own company." I replied, "Well, you know, all the boys in other companies are the same to me as those in my Company E; you are all doing the same duty, and I will do just the same for you." "Yes," they would say, "we know that, because you were the first woman we saw when we came into camp, and you took an interest in us boys ever since we have been here, and we are very grateful for all you do for us."

When at Camp Shaw, I visited the hospital in Beaufort, where I met Clara Barton. There were a number of sick and wounded soldiers there, and I went often to see the comrades. Miss Barton was always very cordial toward me, and I honored her for her devotion and care of those men.

There was a man, John Johnson, who with his family was taken by our regiment at Edisto. This man afterwards worked in the hospital and was well known to Miss Barton. I have been told since that when she went South, in 1883, she tried to look this man up, but learned he was dead.

His son is living in Edisto, Rev. J. J. Johnson, and is the president of an industrial school on that island and a very intelligent man. He was a small child when his father and family were captured by our regiment at Edisto.

VI

ON MORRIS AND OTHER ISLANDS

ORT WAGNER BEING ONLY A MILE from our camp, I went there two or three times a week, and would go up on the ramparts to watch the gunners send their shells into Charleston (which they did every fifteen minutes), and had a full view of the city from that point. Outside of the fort were many skulls lying about; I have often moved them one side out of the path. The comrades and I would have quite a debate as to which side the men fought on. Some thought they were the skulls of our boys; others thought they were the enemy's; but as there was no definite way to know, it was never decided which could lay claim to them. They were a gruesome sight, those fleshless heads and grinning jaws, but by this time I had become accustomed to worse things and did not feel as I might have earlier in my camp life.

It seems strange how our aversion to seeing suffering is overcome in war—how we are able to see the most sickening sights, such as men with their limbs blown off and mangled by the deadly shells, without a shudder; and instead of turning away, how we hurry to assist in alleviating their pain, bind up their wounds, and press the cool water to their parched lips, with feelings only of sympathy and pity.

About the first of June, 1864, the regiment was ordered to Folly Island, staying there until the latter part of the month, when it was ordered to Morris Island. We landed on Morris Island between June and July, 1864. This island was a narrow strip of sandy soil, nothing growing on it but a few bushes and shrubs. The camp was one mile from the boat landing, called Pawnell Landing, and the landing one mile from Fort Wagner.

Colonel Higginson had left us in May of this year, on account of wounds received at Edisto. All the men were sorry to lose him. They did not want him to go, they loved him so. He was kind and devoted to his men, thoughtful for their comfort, and we missed his genial presence from the camp.

The regiment under Colonel Trowbridge did garrison duty, but they had troublesome times from Fort Gregg, on James Island, for the rebels would throw a shell over on our island every now and then. Finally orders were received for the boys to prepare to take Fort Gregg, each man to take 150 rounds of cartridges, canteens of water, hardtack, and salt beef. This order was sent three days prior to starting, to allow them to be in readiness. I helped as many as I could to pack haversacks and cartridge boxes.

The fourth day, about five o'clock in the afternoon, the call was sounded, and I heard the first sergeant say, "Fall in, boys, fall in," and they were not long obeying the command. Each company marched out of its street, in front of their colonel's headquarters, where they rested for half an hour, as it was not dark enough, and they did not want the enemy to have a chance to spy their movements. At the end of this time the line was formed with the 103d New York (white) in the rear, and off they started, eager to get to work. It was quite dark by the time they reached Pawnell Landing. I have never forgotten the good-byes of that day, as they left camp. Colonel Trowbridge said to me as he left, "Good-bye, Mrs. King, take care of yourself if you don't see us again." I went with them as far as the landing, and watched them until they got out of sight, and then I returned to the camp. There was no one at camp but those left on picket and a few disabled soldiers, and one woman, a friend of mine, Mary Shaw, and it was lonesome and sad, now that the boys were gone, some never to return.

Mary Shaw shared my tent that night, and we went to bed, but not to sleep, for the fleas nearly ate us alive. We caught a few, but it did seem, now that the men were gone, that every flea in camp had located my tent, and caused us to vacate. Sleep being out of the question, we sat up the remainder of the night.

About four o'clock, July 2, the charge was made. The

firing could be plainly heard in camp. I hastened down to the landing and remained there until eight o'clock that morning. When the wounded arrived, or rather began to arrive, the first one brought in was Samuel Anderson of our company. He was badly wounded. Then others of our boys, some with their legs off, arm gone, foot off, and wounds of all kinds imaginable. They had to wade through creeks and marshes, as they were discovered by the enemy and shelled very badly. A number of the men were lost, some got fastened in the mud and had to cut off the legs of their pants, to free themselves. The 103d New York suffered the most, as their men were very badly wounded.

My work now began. I gave my assistance to try to alleviate their sufferings. I asked the doctor at the hospital what I could get for them to eat. They wanted soup, but that I could not get; but I had a few cans of condensed milk and some turtle eggs, so I thought I would try to make some custard. I had doubts as to my success, for cooking with turtle eggs was something new to me, but the adage has it, "Nothing ventured, nothing done," so I made a venture and the result was a very delicious custard. This I carried to the men, who enjoyed it very much. My services were given at all times for the comfort of these men. I was on hand to assist whenever needed. I was enrolled as company laundress, but I did very little of it, because I was always busy doing other things through camp, and was employed all the time doing something for the officers and comrades.

After this fight, the regiment did not return to the camp for one month. They were ordered to Cole Island in September, where they remained until October. About November 1, 1864, six companies were detailed to go to Gregg Landing, Port Royal Ferry, and the rebels in some way found out some of our forces had been removed and gave our boys in camp a hard time of it, for several nights. In fact, one night it was thought the boys would have to retreat. The colonel told me to go down to the landing, and if they were obliged to retreat, I could go aboard one of our gunboats. One of the gunboats got in the rear, and began to shell General Beauregard's force, which helped our boys retain their possession.

About November 15, I received a letter from Sergeant King, saying the boys were still lying three miles from Gregg Landing and had not had a fight yet; that the rebels were waiting on them and they on the rebels, and each were holding their own; also that General Sherman had taken Fort McAllister, eight miles from Savannah. After receiving this letter I wanted to get to Beaufort, so I could be near to them and so be able to get news from my husband. November 23 I got a pass for Beaufort. I arrived at Hilton Head about three o'clock next day, but there had been a battle, and a steamer arrived with a number of wounded men; so I could not get a transfer to Beaufort. The doctor wished me to remain over until Monday. I did not want to stay. I was anxious to get off, as I knew no one at Hilton Head.

I must mention a pet pig we had on Cole Island. Colonel

Trowbridge brought into camp, one day, a poor, thin little pig, which a German soldier brought back with him on his return from a furlough. His regiment, the 74th Pennsylvania, was just embarking for the North, where it was ordered to join the 10th corps, and he could not take the pig back with him, so he gave it to our colonel. That pig grew to be the pet of the camp, and was the special care of the drummer boys, who taught him many tricks; and so well did they train him that every day at practice and dress parade, his pigship would march out with them, keeping perfect time with their music. The drummers would often disturb the devotions by riding this pig into the midst of evening praise meeting, and many were the complaints made to the colonel, but he was always very lenient towards the boys, for he knew they only did this for mischief. I shall never forget the fun we had in camp with "Piggie."

VII

CAST AWAY

THERE WAS A YACHT THAT CARRIED passengers from Hilton Head to Beaufort. There were also five small boats which carried people over. The only people here, beside the soldiers, were Mrs. Lizzie Brown, who came over on a permit to see her husband, who was at this place, and was very ill (he died while she was there), Corporal Walker's wife, with her two years old child, and Mrs. Seabrooke. As soon as we could get the yacht, these persons I have mentioned, together with a comrade just discharged, an officer's boy, and myself, took passage on it for Beaufort. It was nearly dark before we had gone any distance, and about eight o'clock we were cast away and were only saved through the mercy of God. I remember going down twice. As I rose the second time, I caught hold of the sail and managed to hold fast. Mrs. Walker held on to her child with one hand, while with the other she managed to hold fast to some part of the boat, and we drifted and shouted as loud as we could, trying to attract the attention of some of the government boats which were going up and down the river. But it was in vain, we could not make ourselves heard, and just when we gave up all hope, and in the last moment (as we thought) gave one more despairing cry, we were heard at Lady's Island. Two boats were put off and a search was made, to locate our distressed boat. They found us at last, nearly dead from exposure. In fact, the poor little baby was dead, although her mother still held her by her clothing, with her teeth. The soldier was drowned, having been caught under the sail and pinned down. The rest of us were saved. I had to be carried bodily, as I was thoroughly exhausted. We were given the best attention that we could get at this place where we were picked up. The men who saved us were surprised when they found me among the passengers, as one of them, William Geary, of Darien, Georgia, was a friend of my husband. His mother lived about two miles from where we were picked up, and she told me she had heard cries for a long time that night, and was very uneasy about it. Finally, she said to her son, "I think some poor souls are cast away." "I don't think so, mother," he replied; "I saw some people going down the river today. You know this is Christmas, and they are having a good time." But she still persisted that these were cries of distress, and not of joy, and begged him to go out and see. So to satisfy her, he went outside and listened, and then he heard them also, and hastened to get the boats off to find us. We were capsized about 8:15 p.m. and it was near midnight when they found us. Next day, they kept a sharp lookout on the beach for anything that might be washed in from the yacht, and got a trunk and several other things. Had the tide been going out, we should have been carried to sea and lost.

I was very ill and under the doctor's care for some time, in Beaufort. The doctor said I ought to have been rolled, as I had swallowed so much water. In January, 1865, I went back to Cole Island, where I could be attended by my doctor, Dr. Miner, who did all in his power to alleviate my suffering, for I was swollen very much. This he reduced and I recovered, but had a severe cough for a long time afterward.

VIII

A FLAG
OF TRUCE

IN OCTOBER, 1864, SIX COMPANIES OF THE regiment were ordered to Gregg Landing, S. C. Captain L. W. Metcalf, of Co. G, was appointed on General Saxton's staff as provost captain, Lieutenant James B. West acting as assistant general. As in some way our mail had been sent over to the Confederate side and their mail to us, Captain Metcalf and Lieutenant West were detailed to exchange these letters under a flag of truce. So, with an escort of six men of the companies at Port Royal Ferry, the flag was unfurled and the message shouted across the river to the Confederates. Captain Metcalf asked them to come over to our side under the protection of our flag of truce. This the Confederates refused to do, having for their excuse that their boat was too far up the river and so they had no way to cross the river to us. They asked Metcalf to cross to them.

He at once ordered his men to "stack arms," the Confederates following suit, and his boys in blue rowed him over, and he delivered the message, after having introduced himself to the rebel officers. One of these officers was Major Jones, of Alabama, the other Lieutenant Scott, of South Carolina. Major Jones was very cordial to our captain, but Lieutenant Scott would not extend his hand, and stood aside, in sullen silence, looking as if he would like to take revenge then and there. Major Jones said to Captain Metcalf, "We have no one to fight for. Should I meet you again, I shall not forget we have met before." With this he extended his hand to Metcalf and bade him good-bye, but Lieutenant Scott stood by and looked as cross as he possibly could. The letters were exchanged, but it seemed a mystery just how those letters got missent to the opposite sides. Captain Metcalf said he did not feel a mite comfortable while he was on the Confederate soil; as for his men, you can imagine their thoughts. I asked them how they felt on the other side, and they said, "We would have felt much better if we had had our guns with us." It was a little risky, for sometimes the flag of truce is not regarded, but even among the enemy there are some good and loyal persons.

Captain Metcalf is still living in Medford. He is 71 years old, and just as loyal to the old flag and the G. A. R. as he was from 1861 to 1866, when he was mustered out. He was a brave captain, a good officer, and was honored and beloved by all in the regiment.

IX

CAPTURE OF CHARLESTON

ON FEBRUARY 28, 1865, THE REMAIN-
der of the regiment were ordered to Charleston,
as there were signs of the rebels evacuating that
city. Leaving Cole Island, we arrived in Charleston between
nine and ten o'clock in the morning, and found the "rebs"
had set fire to the city and fled, leaving women and children
behind to suffer and perish in the flames. The fire had been
burning fiercely for a day and night. When we landed, under
a flag of truce, our regiment went to work assisting the citizens in subduing the flames. It was a terrible scene. For three
or four days the men fought the fire, saving the property and
effects of the people, yet these white men and women could
not tolerate our black Union soldiers, for many of them had
formerly been their slaves; and although these brave men
risked life and limb to assist them in their distress, men and

even women would sneer and molest them whenever they met them.

I had quarters assigned me at a residence on South Battery Street, one of the most aristocratic parts of the city, where I assisted in caring for the sick and injured comrades. After getting the fire under control, the regiment marched out to the race track, where they camped until March 12, when we were ordered to Savannah, Ga. We arrived there on the 13th, about eight o'clock in the evening, and marched out to Fairlong, near the A. & G. R. R., where we remained about ten days, when we were ordered to Augusta, Ga., where Captain Alexander Heasley, of Co. E, was shot and killed by a Confederate. After his death Lieutenant Parker was made captain of the company, and was with us until the regiment was mustered out. He often told me about Massachusetts, but I had no thought at that time that I should ever see that State, and stand in the "Cradle of Liberty."

The regiment remained in Augusta for thirty days, when it was ordered to Hamburg, S. C., and then on to Charleston. It was while on their march through the country, to the latter city, that they came in contact with the bushwhackers (as the rebels were called), who hid in the bushes and would shoot the Union boys every chance they got. Other times they would conceal themselves in the cars used to transfer our soldiers, and when our boys, worn out and tired, would fall asleep, these men would come out from their hiding places and cut their throats. Several of our men were killed in this way, but it could not be found out who was committing these murders until one night one of the rebels was caught in the act, trying to cut the throat of a sleeping soldier. He was put under guard, court-martialed, and shot at Wall Hollow.

First Lieutenant Jerome T. Furman and a number of soldiers were killed by these South Carolina bushwhackers at Wall Hollow. After this man was shot, however, the regiment marched through unmolested to Charleston.

X

MUSTERED
OUT

THE REGIMENT, UNDER COLONEL
Trowbridge, reached Charleston in November,
1865, and camped on the race track until January,
when they returned to Morris Island, and on February 9,
1866, the following "General Orders" were received and the
regiment mustered out.

They were delighted to go home, but oh! How they
hated to part from their commanding chief, Colonel C. T.
Trowbridge. He was the very first officer to take charge of
black soldiers. We thought there was no one like him, for he
was a "man" among his soldiers. All in the regiment knew
him personally, and many were the jokes he used to tell
them. I shall never forget his friendship and kindness toward
me, from the first time I met him to the end of the war.
There was never anyone from the North who came into our
camp but he would bring them to see me.

While on a visit South in 1888, I met a comrade of the regiment, who often said to me, "You up North, Mrs. King, do you ever see Colonel Trowbridge? How I should like to see him! I don't see why he does not come South sometime. Why, I would take a day off and look up all the 'boys' I could find, if I knew he was coming." I knew this man meant what he said, for the men of the regiment knew Colonel Trowbridge first of all the other officers. He was with them on St. Simons and at Camp Saxton. I remember when the company was being formed, we wished Captain C. T. was our captain, because most of the men in Co. E were the men he brought with him from St. Simon, and they were attached to him. He was always jolly and pleasing with all. I remember, when going into Savannah in 1865, he said that he had been there before the war, and told me many things I did not know about the river. Although this was my home, I had never been on it before. No officer in the army was more beloved than our late lieutenant-colonel, C. T. Trowbridge.

[Copy of General Orders.]

"General Orders

"HEADQUARTERS 33D U. S. C. T.,

"LATE 1ST SO. CAROLINA VOLUNTEERS,

"MORRIS ISLAND, S. C., Feb. 9, 1866.

"General Order,
"No. 1.

"COMRADES: The hour is at hand when we must separate forever, and nothing can take from us the pride we feel, when we look upon the history of the 'First South Carolina Volunteers,' the first black regiment that ever bore arms in defense of freedom on the continent of America.

"On the 9th day of May, 1862, at which time there were nearly four millions of your race in bondage, sanctioned by the laws of the land and protected by our flag—on that day, in the face of the floods of prejudice that well-nigh deluged every avenue to manhood and true liberty, you came forth to do battle for your country and kindred.

"For long and weary months, without pay or even the privilege of being recognized as soldiers, you labored on, only to be disbanded and sent to your homes without even a hope of reward, and when our country, necessitated by the deadly struggle with armed traitors, finally granted you the opportunity again to come forth in defense of the nation's life, the alacrity with which you responded to the call gave abundant evidence of your readiness to strike a manly blow for the liberty of your race.

And from that little band of hopeful, trusting, and brave men who gathered at Camp Saxton, on Port Royal Island, in the fall of '62, amidst the terrible prejudices that surrounded us, has grown an army of a hundred and forty thousand black soldiers, whose valor and heroism has won for your race a name which will live as long as the undying pages of history shall endure; and by whose efforts, united with those of the white man, armed rebellion has been conquered, the millions of bondsmen have been emancipated, and the fundamental law of the land has been so altered as to remove forever the possibility of human slavery being established within the borders of redeemed America. The flag of our fathers, restored to its rightful significance, now floats over every foot of our territory, from Maine to California, and beholds only free men! The prejudices which formerly existed against you are well-nigh rooted out.

"Soldiers, you have done your duty and acquitted yourselves like men who, actuated by such ennobling motives, could not fail; and as the result of your fidelity and obedience you have won your freedom, and oh, how great the reward! It seems fitting to me that the last hours of our existence as a regiment should be passed amidst the unmarked graves of your comrades, at Fort

Wagner. Near you rest the bones of Colonel Shaw, buried by an enemy's hand in the same grave with his black soldiers who fell at his side; where in the future your children's children will come on pilgrimages to do homage to the ashes of those who fell in this glorious struggle.

"The flag which was presented to us by the Rev. George B. Cheever and his congregation, of New York City, on the 1st of January, 1863—the day when Lincoln's immortal proclamation of freedom was given to the world—and which you have borne so nobly through the war, is now to be rolled up forever and deposited in our nation's capital. And while there it shall rest, with the battles in which you have participated inscribed upon its folds, it will be a source of pride to us all to remember that it has never been disgraced by a cowardly faltering in the hour of danger, or polluted by a traitor's touch.

"Now that you are to lay aside your arms, I adjure you, by the associations and history of the past, and the love you bear for your liberties, to harbor no feelings of hatred toward your former masters, but to seek in the paths of honesty, virtue, sobriety, and industry, and by a willing obedience to the laws of the land, to grow up to the full stature of American citizens. The church, the schoolhouse, and the right forever to be free are now secured to you, and every prospect before you is full of hope and encouragement. The nation guarantees to you full protection and justice, and will require from you in return that respect for the laws and orderly deportment which will prove to every one your right to all the privileges of freemen. To the officers of the regiment I would say, your toils are ended, your mission is fulfilled, and we separate forever. The fidelity, patience, and patriotism with which you have discharged your duties to your men and to your country entitle you to a far higher tribute than any words of thankfulness which I can give you from the bottom of my heart. You will find your reward in the proud conviction that the cause for which you have battled so nobly has been crowned with abundant success.

"Officers and soldiers of the 33d U. S. Colored Troops, once the First So. Carolina Volunteers, I bid you all farewell!

"By order of
　　"LT. COLONEL C. T. TROWBRIDGE,
　　　　　　　"Commanding regiment.
　　　　　　　　　　"E. W. HYDE,
　　"1st Lieut. 33d U. S. C. T. and acting adjutant."

I have one of the original copies of these orders still in my possession.

My dear friends! Do we understand the meaning of war? Do we know or think of that war of '61? No, we do not, only those brave soldiers, and those who had occasion to be in it, can realize what it was. I can and shall never forget that terrible war until my eyes close in death. The scenes are just as fresh in my mind today as in '61. I see now each scene—the roll-call, the drum tap, "lights out," the call at night when there was danger from the enemy, the double force of pickets, the cold and rain. How anxious I would be, not knowing what would happen before morning! Many times I would dress, not sure but all would be captured. Other times I would stand at my tent door and try to see what was going on, because night was the time the rebels would try to get into our lines and capture some of the boys. It was mostly at night that our men went out for their scouts, and often had a hand to hand fight with the rebels, and although our men came out sometimes with a few killed or wounded, none of them ever were captured.

We do not, as the black race, properly appreciate the old veterans, white or black, as we ought to. I know what they went through, especially those black men, for the Confederates had no mercy on them; neither did they show any toward the white Union soldiers. I have seen the terrors of that war. I was the wife of one of those men who did not get a penny for eighteen months for their services, only their rations and clothing.

I cannot praise General David Hunter too highly, for he was the first man to arm the black man, in the beginning of 1862. He had a hard struggle to hold all the southern division, with so few men, so he applied to Congress; but the answer to him was, "Do not bother us," which was very discouraging. As the general needed more men to protect the islands and do garrison duty, he organized two companies.

I look around now and see the comforts that our younger generation enjoy, and think of the blood that was shed to make these comforts possible for them, and see how little some of them appreciate the old soldiers. My heart burns within me, at this want of appreciation. There are only a few of them left now, so let us all, as the ranks close, take a deeper interest in them. Let the younger generation take an interest also, and remember that it was through the efforts of these veterans that they and we older ones enjoy our liberty today.

XI

AFTER
THE WAR

IN 1866, THE STEAMERS WHICH RAN FROM Savannah to Darien would not take colored people unless they stayed in a certain part of the boat, away from the white people; so some of the colored citizens and ex-soldiers decided to form a syndicate and buy a steamer of their own. They finally bought a large one of a New York company. It arrived in fine shape, apparently, and made its first trip to Darien. The next trip was to Beaufort. I went on this trip, as the pilot, James Cook, was a friend of my family, and I thought I would enjoy the trip; and I did, getting back in safety. The next trip was to go to Florida, but it never reached there, for on the way down the boat ran upon St. John bar and went entirely to pieces. They found out afterwards that they had been swindled, as the boat was a condemned one, and the company took advantage of them; and as they carried no insurance on the boat they lost all the money they had invested in it. The best people of the city expressed great sympathy for them in their loss, as it promised to prove a great investment at first.

At the close of the war, my husband and I returned to Savannah, a number of the comrades returning at the same time. A new life was before us now, all the old life left behind. After getting settled, I opened a school at my home on South Broad Street, now called Oglethorpe Avenue, as there was not any public school for negro children. I had twenty children at my school, and received one dollar a month for each pupil. I also had a few older ones who came at night. There were several other private schools besides mine. Mrs. Lucinda Jackson had one on the same street I lived on.

I taught almost a year, when the Beach Institute opened, which took a number of my scholars, as this was a free school. On September 16, 1866, my husband, Sergeant King, died, leaving me soon to welcome a little stranger alone. He was a boss carpenter, but being just mustered out of the army, and the prejudice against his race being still too strong to insure him much work at his trade, he took contracts for unloading vessels, and hired a number of men to assist him. He was much respected by the citizens, and was a general favorite with his associates.

In December, 1866, I was obliged to give up teaching, but in April, 1867, I opened a school in Liberty County, Georgia, and taught there one year; but country life did not agree with me, so I returned to the city, and Mrs. Susie Carrier took charge of my school.

On my return to Savannah, I found that the free school had taken all my former pupils, so I opened a night school, where I taught a number of adults. This, together with other things I could get to do and the assistance of my brother-in-law, supported me. I taught this school until the fall of 1868, when a free night school opened at the Beach Institute, and again my scholars left me to attend this free school. So I had to close my school. I put my baby with my mother and entered in the employ of a family, where I lived quite a while, but had to leave, as the work was too hard.

In 1872 I put in a claim for my husband's bounty and received one hundred dollars, some of which I put in the Freedman's Savings Bank. In the fall of 1872 I went to work for a very wealthy lady, Mrs. Charles Green, as laundress. In the spring of 1873, Mr. and Mrs. Green came North to Rye Beach for the summer, and as their cook did not care to go so far from home, I went with them in her place. While there, I won a prize for excellent cooking at a fair which the ladies who were summering there had held to raise funds to build an Episcopal Church, and Mrs. Green was one of the energetic workers to make this fair a success; and it was a success in every respect and a tidy sum was netted.

I returned South with Mrs. Green, and soon after, she went to Europe. I returned to Boston again in 1874, through the kindness of Mrs. Barnard, a daughter of ex-Mayor Otis of Boston. She was accompanied by her husband, Mr. James Barnard (who was an agent for the line of steamers), her six children, the nurse, and myself. We left Savannah on the steamship *Seminole*, under Captain Matthews, and when we had passed Hatteras some distance, she broke her shaft. The captain had the sails hoisted and we drifted along, there being a stiff breeze, which was greatly in our favor. Captain Matthews said the nearest point he could make was Cape Henry Light. About noon, Mr. Barnard spied the light and told the captain if he would give him a boat and some of the crew, he would row to the light for help. This was done, the boat was manned, and they put off. They made the light, then they made for Norfolk, which was eight miles from the light, and did not reach the city until eight o'clock that night.

Next morning he returned with a tug, to tow us into Norfolk for repairs; but the tug was too small to move the steamer, so it went back for more help, but before it returned, a Norfolk steamer, on its way to Boston, stopped to see what was the matter with our steamer. Our trouble was explained to them, and almost all the passengers were transferred to this steamer. Mr. Barnard remained on the steamer, and Mrs. Barnard deciding to remain with him, I went aboard this other steamer with the rest of the passengers. We left them at anchor, waiting for the tugs to return.

This accident brought back very vividly the time previous to this, when I was in that other wreck in 1864, and I wondered if they would reach port safe, for it is a terrible thing to be cast away; but on arriving in Boston, about two days later, I was delighted to hear of the arrival of their steamer at T Wharf, with all on board safe.

Soon after I got to Boston, I entered the service of Mr. Thomas Smith's family, on Walnut Avenue, Boston Highlands, where I remained until the death of Mrs. Smith. I next lived with Mrs. Gorham Gray, Beacon Street, where I remained until I was married, in 1879, to Russell L. Taylor.

In 1880 I had another experience in steamer accidents. Mr. Taylor and I started for New York on the steamer *Stonington*. We were in bed when, sometime in the night, the *Narragansett* collided with our boat. I was awakened by the crash. I was in the ladies' cabin. There were about thirty-five or forty others in the cabin. I sprang out of my berth, dressed as quickly as I could, and tried to reach the deck, but we found the cabin door locked, and two men stood outside and would not let us out. About twenty minutes after, they opened the doors and we went up on deck, and a terrible scene was before us. The *Narragansett* was on fire, in a bright blaze; the water was lighted as far as one could see, the passengers shrieking, groaning, running about, leaping into the water, panic-stricken. A steamer came to our assistance; they put the life-rafts off and saved a great many from the burning steamer, and picked a number up from the water. A colored man saved his wife and child by giving each a chair and having them jump overboard. These chairs kept them afloat until they were taken aboard by the life-raft. The steamer was burned to the water's edge.

The passengers on board our steamer were transferred to another one and got to New York at 9:30 the next morning. A number of lives were lost in this accident, and the bow of the *Stonington* was badly damaged. I was thankful for my escape, for I had been in two similar experiences and got off safely, and I have come to the conclusion I shall never have a watery grave.

XII

THE WOMEN'S
RELIEF CORPS

ALL THIS TIME MY INTEREST IN THE boys in blue had not abated. I was still loyal and true, whether they were black or white. My hands have never left undone anything they could do towards their aid and comfort in the twilight of their lives. In 1886 I helped to organize Corps 67, Women's Relief Corps, auxiliary to the G. A. R., and it is a very flourishing corps today. I have been Guard, Secretary, Treasurer for three years, and in 1893 I was made President of this corps, Mrs. Emily Clark being Department President this year. In 1896, in response to an order sent out by the Department W. R. C. to take a census to secure a complete roster of the Union Veterans of the war of the Rebellion now residing in Massachusetts, I was allotted the West End district, which (with the assistance of Mrs. Lizzie L. Johnson, a member of Corps 67, and widow of a soldier of the 54th Mass. Volunteers) I canvassed with splendid success, and found a great many comrades who were not attached to any post in the city or State.

In 1898 the Department of Mass. W. R. C. gave a grand fair at Music Hall. I made a large quilt of red, white, and blue ribbon that made quite a sensation. The quilt was voted for and was awarded to the Department President, Mrs. E. L. W. Waterman, of Boston.

XIII

THOUGHTS ON PRESENT CONDITIONS

LIVING HERE IN BOSTON WHERE THE black man is given equal justice, I must say a word on the general treatment of my race, both in the North and South, in this twentieth century. I wonder if our white fellow men realize the true sense or meaning of brotherhood? For two hundred years we had toiled for them; the war of 1861 came and was ended, and we thought our race was forever freed from bondage, and that the two races could live in unity with each other, but when we read almost every day of what is being done to my race by some whites in the South, I sometimes ask, "Was the war in vain? Has it brought freedom, in the full sense of the word, or has it not made our condition more hopeless?"

In this "land of the free" we are burned, tortured, and denied a fair trial, murdered for any imaginary wrong conceived in the brain of the negro-hating white man. There is no redress for us from a government which promised to protect all under its flag. It seems a mystery to me. They say, "One flag, one nation, one country indivisible." Is this true? Can we say this truthfully, when one race is allowed to burn, hang, and inflict the most horrible torture weekly, monthly, on another? No, we cannot sing "My country, 'tis of thee, Sweet land of Liberty"! It is hollow mockery. The Southland laws are all on the side of the white, and they do just as they like to the negro, whether in the right or not.

I do not uphold my race when they do wrong. They ought to be punished, but the innocent are made to suffer as well as the guilty, and I hope the time will hasten when it will be stopped forever. Let us remember God says, "He that sheds blood, his blood shall be required again." I may not live to see it, but the time is approaching when the South will again have cause to repent for the blood it has shed of innocent black men, for their blood cries out for vengeance. For the South still cherishes a hatred toward the blacks, although there are some true Southern gentlemen left who abhor the stigma brought upon them, and feel it very keenly, and I hope the day is not far distant when the two races will reside in peace in the Southland, and we will sing with sincere and truthful hearts, "My country, 'tis of thee, Sweet land of Liberty, of thee I sing."

I have been in many States and cities, and in each I have looked for liberty and justice, equal for the black as for the white; but it was not until I was within the borders of New England, and reached old Massachusetts, that I found it. Here is found liberty in the full sense of the word, liberty for the stranger within her gates, irrespective of race or creed, liberty and justice for all.

We have before us still another problem to solve. With the close of the Spanish war, and on the entrance of the Americans into Cuba, the same conditions confront us as the war of 1861 left. The Cubans are free, but it is a limited freedom, for prejudice, deep-rooted, has been brought to them and a separation made between the white and black Cubans, a thing that had never existed between them before; but today there is the same intense hatred toward the negro in Cuba that there is in some parts of this country.

I helped to furnish and pack boxes to be sent to the soldiers and hospitals during the first part of the Spanish war; there were black soldiers there too. At the battle of San Juan Hill, they were in the front, just as brave, loyal, and true as those other black men who fought for freedom and the right; and yet their bravery and faithfulness were reluctantly acknowledged, and praise grudgingly given. All we ask for is "equal justice," the same that is accorded to all other races who come to this country, of their free will (not forced to, as we were), and are allowed to enjoy every privilege, unrestricted, while we are denied what is rightfully our own in a country which the labor of our forefathers helped to make what it is.

One thing I have noticed among my people in the South: they have accumulated a large amount of real estate, far surpassing the colored owners in the North, who seem to let their opportunity slip by them. Nearly all of Brownsville (a suburb of Savannah) is owned by colored people, and so it is in a great many other places throughout the State, and all that is needed is the protection of the law as citizens.

In 1867, soon after the death of my father, who had served on a gunboat during the war, my mother opened a grocery store, where she kept general merchandise always on hand. These she traded for cash or would exchange for crops of cotton, corn, or rice, which she would ship once a month, to F. Lloyd & Co., or Johnson & Jackson, in Savannah. These were colored merchants, doing business on Bay Street in that city. Mother bought her first property, which contained ten acres. She next purchased fifty acres of land. Then she had a chance to get a place with seven hundred acres of land, and she bought this.

In 1870, Colonel Hamilton and Major Devendorft, of Oswego, N.Y., came to the town and bought up a tract of land at a place called Doctortown, and started a mill. Mrs. Devendorft heard of my mother and went to see her, and persuaded her to come to live with her, assuring her she would be as one of the family. Mother went with her, but after a few months she went to Doctortown, where she has been since, and now owns the largest settlement there. All trains going to Florida pass her place, just across the Altamaha River. She is well known by both white and black; the people are fond of her, and will not allow anyone to harm her.

Mr. Devendorft sold out his place in 1880 and went back to New York, where later he died.

I read an article, which said the ex-Confederate Daughters had sent a petition to the managers of the local theatres in Tennessee to prohibit the performance of *Uncle Tom's Cabin*, claiming it was exaggerated (that is, the treatment of the slaves), and would have a very bad effect on the children who might see the drama. I paused and thought back a few years of the heart-rending scenes I have witnessed; I have seen many times, when I was a mere girl, thirty or forty men, handcuffed, and as many women and children, come every first Tuesday of each month from Mr. Wiley's trade office to the auction blocks, one of them being situated on Drayton Street and Court Lane, the other on Bryant Street, near the Pulaski House. The route was down our principal street, Bull Street, to the courthouse, which was only a block from where I resided.

All people in those days got all their water from the city pumps, which stood about a block apart throughout the city. The one we used to get water from was opposite the courthouse, on Bull Street. I remember, as if it were yesterday, seeing droves of negroes going to be sold, and I often went to look at them, and I could hear the auctioneer very plainly from my house, auctioning these poor people off.

Do these Confederate Daughters ever send petitions to

prohibit the atrocious lynchings and wholesale murdering and torture of the negro? Do you ever hear of them fearing this would have a bad effect on the children? Which of these two, the drama or the present state of affairs, makes a degrading impression upon the minds of our young generation? In my opinion it is not *Uncle Tom's Cabin*, but it should be the one that has caused the world to cry "Shame!" It does not seem as if our land is yet civilized. It is like times long past, when rulers and high officers had to flee for their lives, and the negro has been dealt with in the same way since the war by those he lived with and toiled for two hundred years or more. I do not condemn all the Caucasian race because the negro is badly treated by a few of the race. No! For had it not been for the true whites, assisted by God and the prayers of our forefathers, I should not be here today.

There are still good friends to the negro. Why, there are still thousands that have not bowed to Baal. So it is with us. Man thinks two hundred years is a long time, and it is, too; but it is only as a week to God, and in his own time—I know I shall not live to see the day, but it will come—the South will be like the North, and when it comes it will be prized higher than we prize the North today. God is just; when he created man he made him in his image, and never intended one should misuse the other. All men are born free and equal in his sight.

I am pleased to know at this writing that the officers and comrades of my regiment stand ready to render me assistance whenever required. It seems like "bread cast upon the water," and it has returned after many days, when it is most needed. I have received letters from some of the comrades, since we parted in 1866, with expressions of gratitude and thanks to me for teaching them their first letters. One of them, Peter Waggall, is a minister in Jacksonville, Fla. Another is in the government service at Washington, D. C. Others are in Darien and Savannah, Ga., and all are doing well.

There are many people who do not know what some of the colored women did during the war. There were hundreds of them who assisted the Union soldiers by hiding them and helping them to escape. Many were punished for taking food to the prison stockades for the prisoners. When I went into Savannah, in 1865, I was told of one of these stockades which was in the suburbs of the city, and they said it was an awful place. The Union soldiers were in it, worse than pigs, without any shelter from sun or storm, and the colored women would take food there at night and pass it to them, through the holes in the fence. The soldiers were starving, and these women did all they could towards relieving those men, although they knew the penalty, should they be caught giving them aid. Others assisted in various ways the Union Army. These things should be kept in history before the people. There has never been a greater war in the United States than the one of 1861, where so many lives were lost—not men alone but noble women as well.

Let us not forget that terrible war, or our brave soldiers who were thrown into Andersonville and Libby prisons, the awful agony they went through, and the most brutal treatment they received in those loathsome dens, the worst ever given human beings; and if the white soldiers were subjected to such treatment, what must have been the horrors inflicted on the negro soldiers in their prison pens? Can we forget those cruelties? No, though we try to forgive and say, "No North, no South," and hope to see it in reality before the last comrade passes away.

XIV

A VISIT TO LOUISIANA

THE INEVITABLE ALWAYS HAPPENS. On February 3, 1898, I was called to Shreveport, La., to the bedside of my son, who was very ill. He was traveling with Nickens and Company, with *The Lion's Bride*, when he fell ill, and had been ill two weeks when they sent to me. I tried to have him brought home to Boston, but they could not send him, as he was not able to sit and ride this long distance; so on the sixth of February I left Boston to go to him. I reached Cincinnati on the eighth, where I took the train for the South. I asked a white man standing near (before I got my train) what car I should take. "Take that one," he said, pointing to one. "But that is a smoking car!" "Well," he replied, "that is the car for colored people." I went to this car, and on entering it all my courage failed me. I have ridden in many coaches, but I was never in such as these. I wanted to return home again, but when I thought of my sick boy I said, "Well, others ride in these cars and I must do likewise," and tried to be resigned, for I wanted to reach my boy, as I did not know whether I should find him alive. I arrived in Chattanooga at eight o'clock in the evening, where the porter took my baggage to the train which was to leave for Marion, Miss. Soon after I was seated, just before the train pulled out, two tall men with slouch hats on walked through the car, and on through the train. Finally they came back to our car and stopping at my seat said, "Where are those men who were with you?" I did not know to whom they were speaking, as there was another woman in the car, so I made no reply. Again they asked me, standing directly in front of my seat, "Where are those men who came in with you?" "Are you speaking to me?" I said. "Yes!" they said. "I have not seen any men," I replied. They looked at me a moment, and one of them asked where I was from. I told him Boston; he hesitated a minute and walked out of our car to the other car.

When the conductor came around I told him what these men had said, and asked him if they allowed persons to enter the car and insult passengers. He only smiled. Later, when the porter came in, I mentioned it to him. He said, "Lady, I see you do not belong here; where are you from?" I told him. He said, "I have often heard of Massachusetts. I want to see that place." "Yes!" I said. "You can ride there on the cars, and no person would be allowed to speak to you as those men did to me." He explained that those men were constables, who were in search of a man who had eloped with another man's wife. "That is the way they do here. Each morning you can hear of some negro being lynched;" and on seeing my surprise, he said, "Oh, that is nothing; it is done all the time. We have no rights here. I have been on this road for fifteen years and have seen some terrible things." He wanted to know what I was doing down there, and I told him it was only the illness of my son that brought me there.

I was a little surprised at the way the poor whites were made to ride on this road. They put them all together by themselves in a car, between the colored people's coach and the first-class coach, and it looked like the "laborers' car" used in Boston to carry the different day laborers to and from their work.

I got to Marion, Miss., at two o'clock in the morning, arrived at Vicksburg at noon, and at Shreveport about eight o'clock in the evening, and found my son just recovering from a severe hemorrhage. He was very anxious to come home, and I tried to secure a berth for him on a sleeper, but they would not sell me one, and he was not strong enough to travel otherwise. If I could only have gotten him to Cincinnati, I might have brought him home, but as I could not I was forced to let him remain where he was. It seemed very hard, when his father fought to protect the Union and our flag, and yet his boy was denied, under this same flag, a berth to carry him home to die, because he was a negro.

Shreveport is a little town, made up largely of Jews and

Germans and a few Southerners, the negroes being in the majority. Its sidewalks are sand except on the main street. Almost all the stores are kept either by the Jews or Germans. They know a stranger in a minute, as the town is small and the citizens know each other; if not personally, their faces are familiar.

I went into a jewelry store one day to have a crystal put in my watch, and the attendant remarked, "You are a stranger." I asked him how he knew that. He said he had watched me for a week or so. I told him yes, I was a stranger and from Boston. "Oh! I have heard of Boston," he said. "You will not find this place like it is there. How do you like this town?" "Not very well," I replied.

I found that the people who had lived in Massachusetts and were settled in Shreveport were very cordial to me and glad to see me. There was a man murdered in cold blood for nothing. He was a colored man and a "porter" in a store in this town. A clerk had left his umbrella at home. It had begun to rain when he started for home, and on looking for the umbrella he could not, of course, find it. He asked the porter if he had seen it. He said no, he had not. "You answer very saucy," said the clerk, and drawing his revolver, he shot the colored man dead. He was taken up the street to an office where he was placed under one thousand dollars bond for his appearance and released, and that was the end of the case. I was surprised at this, but I was told by several white and colored persons that this was a common occurrence, and the persons were never punished if they were white, but no mercy was shown to negroes.

I met several comrades, white and colored, there, and noticed that the colored comrades did not wear their buttons. I asked one of them why this was, and was told, should they wear it, they could not get work. Still some would wear their buttons in spite of the feeling against it. I met a newsman from New York on the train. He was a veteran, and said that Sherman ought to come back and go into that part of the country.

Shreveport is a horrid place when it rains. The earth is red and sticks to your shoes, and it is impossible to keep rubbers on, for the mud pulls them off. Going across the Mississippi River, I was amazed to see how the houses were built, so close to the shore, or else on low land; and when the river rises, it flows into these houses and must make it very disagreeable and unhealthy for the inmates.

After the death of my son, while on my way back to Boston, I came to Clarksdale, one of the stations on the road from Vicksburg. In this town a Mr. Hancock, of New York, had a large cotton plantation, and the Chinese intermarry with the blacks.

At Clarksdale, I saw a man hanged. It was a terrible sight, and I felt alarmed for my own safety down there. When I reached Memphis I found conditions of travel much better. The people were mostly Western and Northern here; the cars were nice, but separate for colored persons until we reached the Ohio River, when the door was opened and the porter passed through, saying, "The Ohio River! Change to the other car." I thought, "What does he mean? We have been riding all this distance in separate cars, and now we are all to sit together." It certainly seemed a peculiar arrangement. Why not let the negroes, if their appearance and respectability warrant it, be allowed to ride as they do in the North, East, or West?

There are others beside the blacks, in the South and North, that should be put in separate cars while traveling, just as they put my race. Many black people in the South do not wish to be thrown into a car because all are colored, as there are many of their race very objectionable to them, being of an entirely different class; but they have to adapt themselves to the circumstances and ride with them, because they are all negroes. There is no such division with the whites. Except in one place I saw, the workingman and the millionaire ride in the same coaches together. Why not allow the respectable, law-abiding classes of the blacks the same privilege? We hope for better conditions in the future, and feel sure they will come in time, surely if slowly.

While in Shreveport, I visited ex-Senator Harper's house. He is a colored man and owns a large business block, besides a fine residence on Cado Street and several good building lots. Another family, the Pages, living on the same street, were quite wealthy, and a large number of colored families owned their homes, and were industrious, refined people; and if they were only allowed justice, the South would be the only place for our people to live.

We are similar to the children of Israel, who, after many weary years in bondage, were led into that land of promise, there to thrive and be forever free from persecution; and I don't despair, for the Book which is our guide through life declares, "Ethiopia shall stretch forth her hand."

What a wonderful revolution! In 1861 the Southern papers were full of advertisements for "slaves," but now, despite all the hindrances and "race problems," my people are striving to attain the full standard of all other races born free in the sight of God, and in a number of instances have succeeded. Justice we ask—to be citizens of these United States, where so many of our people have shed their blood with their white comrades, that the stars and stripes should never be polluted.

APPENDIX

ROSTER OF SURVIVORS OF THIRTY-THIRD UNITED STATES COLORED TROOPS

THE following are the names of officers and men as near as I have been able to reach.

Colonel T. W. Higginson.
Lieut.-Col. C. T. Trowbridge.

COMPANY A.

Capt. Charles E. Parker,
Lieut. John A. Trowbridge,
Lieut. J. B. West,
O.-Sergt. Joseph Holden,
1st Sergt.——Hattent,
2d Sergt. Wm. Jackson,
Thomas Smith,
George Green,
Manly Gater,
Paul Jones,
Sancho Jenkins,
London Bailey,
Edmund Mack,

Andrew Perry,
Morris Williams,
James Dorsen,
Abel Haywood.

COMPANY B.

Capt. Wm. James,
O.-Sergt. Bob Bowling,
2d Sergt. Nathan Hagans,
3d Sergt. Cato Wright,
4th Sergt. Frederick Parker,
5th Sergt. Wm. Simmons,
Corp. Monday Stewart,
Corp. Allick Seymore,
Corp. Lazarus Fields,
Corp. Boson Green,
Corp. Steven Wright,
Corp. Carolina Hagans,
Corp. Richard Robinson,
David Hall,
Edward Houston,
Smart Givins,
John Mills,
Jacob Riley,
Frederick Procter,
Benj. Gordon,
Benj. Mason,

Sabe Natteal,
Joseph Noyels,
Benj. Mackwell,
Thos. Hernandes,
Israel Choen,
Steplight Gordon,
Chas. Talbert,
Isaac Jenkins,
Morris Polite,
Robert Freeman,
Jacob Watson,
Benj. Managualt,
Richard Adams,
Mingo Singleton,
Toney Chapman,
Jos. Knowell,
Benj. Gardner.

COMPANY C.

Capt. A. W. Jackson,
2d Sergt. Billy Milton,
Corp. Peter Waggall,
Corp. Henry Abrams,
Martin Dickson, Drummer,
Roddrick Langs, Fifer,
Joseph Smith,
Solomon Major,

John Brown,
Bram Strowbridge,
Robert Trewell,
Jerry Fields,
Paul Fields,
William Johnson,
Bram Stoved,
Robert Mack,
Samuel Mack,
Jack Mack,
Simon Gatson,
Bob Bolden,
James Long,
O.-S. Frederick Brown.

COMPANY D.

Sergt. Isaiah Brown,
Luke Wright,
Dick Haywood,
Stephen Murrel,
Jos. Halsley,
Nathan Hazeby,
O.-Sergt. Robert Godwen,
Peter Johnson,
Cæsar Johnson,
Sampson Cuthbert.

COMPANY E.

Capt. N. G. Parker,
Corp. Jack Sallens,
Quaker Green,
Abram Fuller,
Levan Watkins,
Peter Chisholm,
Scipio Haywood,
Paul King,
Richard Howard,
Esau Kellison,
Chas. Armstrong,
Washington Demry,
Benj. King,
Luke Harris,
William Cummings.

COMPANY F.

Capt. John Thompson,
Sergt. Robert Vandross,
Sergt. Cæsar Alston,
2d Sergt. Moses Green,
Corp. Samuel Mack,
Edmund Washington,
Isaac Jenkins,
Chas. Seymore,

Frank Grayson,
Bristow Eddy,
Abram Fields,
Joseph Richardson,
James Brown,
Frederick Tripp,
Frost Coleman,
Paul Coleman,
Robert Edward,
Milton Edward.

COMPANY G.

Capt. L. W. Metcalf,
Sergt. T. W. Long,
Corp. Prince Logan,
Corp. Mark Clark,
Corp. James Ash,
Corp. Henry Hamilton,
Roddrick Long,
Benjamin Turner,
David Wanton,
Benjamin Martin,
John Ryals,
Charles Williams,
Hogarth Williams,
Benjamin Wright,
Henry Harker.

COMPANY H.

Capt. W. W. Sampson,
1st Sergt. Jacob Jones,
2d Sergt. Thomas Fields,
Corp. A. Brown,
Corp. Emmanuel Washington,
Jackson Danner,
Joseph Wright,
Phillips Brown,
Luke Harris,
Lazarus Aikens,
Jonah Aikens,
Jacob Jones,
Thomas Howard,
William Williams,
Jack Parker,
Jack Ladson,
Poll McKee,
Lucius Baker.

COMPANY I.

2d Sergt. Daniel Spaulding,
Corp. Uandickpe,
Corp. Floward,
Corp. Thompson.

COMPANY K.

O.-Sergt. Harry Williams,
2d Sergt. Billy Coleman,
3d Sergt. Cæsar Oston,
Jacob Lance,
Jack Burns,
Wm. McLean,
Geo. Washington,
David Wright,
Jerry Mitchell,
Jackson Green,
David Putnam,
B. Lance,
Ward McKen,
Edmond Cloud,
Chance Mitchel,
Leon Simmons,
Prince White,
Stephen Jenkins.

Quarter-Master Harry West.
Quarter-Master's Sergt., Edward Colvin.

A LIST OF THE BATTLES
FOUGHT BY THE THIRTY-THIRD
U. S. COLORED TROOPS, FORMERLY
FIRST S. C. VOLUNTEERS

Darien, Ga., and Ridge 1862

St. Mary's River and Hundred Pines 1862

Pocotaligo Bridge[1] 1862

Jacksonville, Fla 1863

Township. 1863

Mill Town Bluff[2] 1863

Hall Island 1863

Johns Island 1863

Coosaw River. 1863

Combahee and Edisto[3] 1863

James Island[4] 1864

Honey Hill. 1864

[1] Many prisoners and stores captured.
[2] Four prisoners captured.
[3] 300 prisoners captured.
[4] Fort Gregg captured.